Collins

Aiming for Level
Reading

4

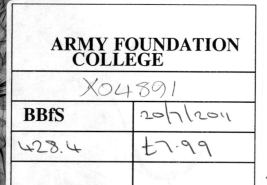

Caroline Bentley-Davies

Gareth Calway

Nicola Copitch

Steve Eddy

Najoud Ensaff

Matthew Tett

Series editor: Gareth Calway

Published by Collins
An imprint of HarperCollins Publishers
77-85 Fulham Palace Road
Hammersmith
London
W6 8JB

Browse the complete Collins catalogue at
www.collinseducation.com

© HarperCollins Publishers Limited 2009

10 9 8 7 6 5 4 3 2
ISBN 978 0 00 731356 3

Caroline Bentley-Davies, Gareth Calway, Nicola Copitch, Steve Eddy, Najoud Ensaff and Matthew Tett assert their moral rights to be identified as the authors of this work.

British Library Cataloguing in Publication Data.
A Catalogue record for this publication is available from the British Library.

Commissioning by Catherine Martin
Design and typesetting by Jordan Publishing Design
Cover Design by Angela English
Printed and bound by Printing Express, Hong Kong

Acknowledgements

Slimbridge Wetland Centre, pp6, 12; The London Dungeons, p13; WaterAid brochure courtesy of WaterAid, p14; RSPCA brochure courtesy of the RSPCA, p15; 'Love thy Neighbour' 9 October 2008 with permission of The Daily Mirror, pp18–9; 'Zac Who?' *The Daily Mail* (8 October 2008, page 11) reproduced with permission of Solo Syndication, p20; Extract from *In the Middle of the Night* by Robert Cormier. Reprinted by permission of HarperCollins Publishers © Robert Cormier 1996, pp22, 24, 25; Blurb and cover of *The Trap* by John Smelcer, courtesy of Andersen Press Ltd., p27; Encyclopaedia page from the *Collins Dictionary of Science* Reproduced with permission of HarperCollins Publishers, p32; Lazer Zone leaflet courtesy of Laser Zone, Scarborough, p34;

Robin Hood leaflet courtesy of The Tales of Robin Hood, Nottingham, p35; Ian Serraillier, 'Locking Up' courtesy of Oxford University Press, p41; Katherine Langrish, *Troll Fell*. Reprinted by permission of HarperCollins Publishers Ltd © Katherine Langrish 2004, p46; *The Kingdom by the Sea* by Robert Westall Reprinted by permission of HarperCollins Publishers Ltd © Robert Westall 2001, p48; *Cirque du Freak* by Darren Shan. Reprinted by permission of HarperCollins Publishers Ltd © Darren Shan, 2000, p49; *Dosh* by Robert Swindles. Reprinted by permission of Longman Publishers, p50; Extract from *The Boy in the Striped Pyjamas* by John Boyne, published by David Fickling Books. Reprinted by permission of The Random House Group Ltd., p.59; Extract from APACHE by Tanya Landman. Apache © 2007 Tanya Landman.; Reproduced by permission of WALKER Books Ltd, London SE11 5HJ, p68; Extract from *King of Shadows* by Susan Cooper, published by Bodley Head Children's Books. Reprinted by permission of The Random House Group Ltd., p69; Extract from *And Then There Were None* by Agatha Christie. Reprinted by permission of HarperCollins Publishers Ltd ©Agatha Christie, p70; Extracts from The Murder of Roger Ackroyd by Agatha Christie. Reproduced by permission of HarperCollins Publishers Ltd., p71; Extract from *Pirates* by Celia Rees reprinted by permission of Bloomsbury, p72; Extract from *Treasure Island* by Ken Ludwig. Reproduced by permission of HarperCollins Publishers and Macnaughton Lord Representation. © Ken Ludwig 2007., p73; Extract from *Apache* by Ed Macy. Reproduced by permission of HarperCollins Publishers Ltd. © Ed Macy 2008.; PGL website pages, courtesy of PGL holidays, pp78–9; 'The Little Smasher' 23 November 2008 with permission of The Observer © Guardian News and Media Limited., p80; Extract from *Forest of Doom* by Jennie Walters, courtesy of Brilliant Books Ltd, p86

The publishers would like to thank the following for permission to reproduce pictures in these pages:

Alamy: p46; BBC Sport website, p33; Black Swan for the front cover of *The Boy in the Striped Pyjamas* by John Boyne, p61; Bridgeman Art Library: The Lion and Albert, 2001 (oil & tempera on panel) by Broomfield, Frances (Contemporary Artist) Private Collection/ © Frances Broomfield / Portal Gallery, London/ The Bridgeman Art Library p62; Corbis: p68; Getty Images: pp20, 51, 62; HarperCollins Publishers pp22, 32; iStockphoto: pp7, 15, 25, 40, 49, 52, 53; Imperial War Museum: p76; KPA/Zuma/Rex Features, p26; Lowry Museum, Manchester for permission to reproduce L.S. Lowry, *Going To Work*, p44; Manchester Art Gallery for *Balaclava* by Elizabeth Butler, p77; Mary Evans Picture Library: p74l; PA Photos: p78, Rex Features: pp10, 26, 30, 74; Ronald Grant Archive: pp9, 51; Safety Services Direct Ltd, p32.

Contents

Chapter 1

AF2 Understand, describe, select or retrieve information, events or ideas from text and use quotation and reference to text

This chapter is going to show you how to

- Find and comment on relevant points in a text
- Select relevant points from a range of sources
- Support your ideas with detail from the text
- Find quotations to support your ideas.

What's it all about?

This chapter teaches you how to select information or ideas from texts. The ability to pick out relevant parts of a text to support your ideas is an important skill.

This lesson will
- show you how to understand the main points in a text.

Mostly when we read a text, we are doing it for a reason: to find out something. Often when we read a text we must decide which are the most important parts.

Getting you thinking

Look at this page from a leaflet about a wildlife centre. It has been written to try to persuade people to visit the centre.

Question: What attractions are there in Slimbridge?

- Find three attractions you can see if you visit Slimbridge.
- Explain what you can do at each attraction.

welcome to
Slimbridge
Wetland Centre

every season brings new visitors

Whatever the time of year or weather there is always something new to see and do.

The award winning visitor centre, is the perfect place to relax and enjoy Slimbridge. Take a trip to the top of the **Sloane Tower** for a magnificent 360 view of Slimbridge and the Severn Estuary, explore the **Discovery Centre** and enjoy wildlife inspired films in the **cinema** and art in the **gallery**.

Take time to relax in the **restaurant** overlooking the **Caribbean Flamingos** and find the perfect gift in the **shop**.

The visitor centre is also home to **activities and events throughout the year,** with a diverse programme which encompasses everything from arts and crafts sessions to bird watching, music festivals to farmers markets. Visit **wwt.org.uk** for further details.

How does it work?

Four attractions are mentioned in the extract. You are also asked to explain what you can do at each place.

You might have said:

1 *There is a tall tower where you can see Slimbridge from 360 degrees.*

2 *There is a Discovery Centre with a cinema where you can watch wildlife-inspired films.*

3 *There is a restaurant where you can watch flamingos while you have lunch.*

Now you try it

Here is a paragraph about vultures. Read the text and then answer the questions below.

Vultures often watch sick animals. They wait for the animals to die so that they can feast on their meat. Vultures eat flesh which includes bone marrow. They eat the bone marrow by swallowing bones. These interesting birds are found in parts of America, Africa, Asia and Southern Europe.

1 Why do vultures watch sick animals?

2 How do vultures eat bone marrow?

3 Name two places where can you find vultures.

Check your progress

LEVEL 3	I can locate some relevant points
LEVEL 4	I can choose relevant points from the text
LEVEL 5	I can select several relevant points and comment on them

This lesson will
- show you how to compare texts.

If we are trying to find out something, we often have to read several different texts on the same topic. To find the information we need, it is important to look for similarities and differences in what these texts are saying.

Getting you thinking

Read the following two reviews of a recent pop album.

- Find one similarity and one difference in the two texts.

A

About Time ★★★★★

It's been almost ten years since Britney Spears' 10 million selling debut album *Baby One More Time* was released.

This girl exploded onto the pop scene with catchy tunes and well written songs. Straight away, everyone from mums to teenage boys loved her stunning good looks and appealing songs.

Since then Britney has hit the headlines as her personal life spiralled out of control and we all wondered if she was too busy to make music again.

But it looks as if Britney has made a fantastic new album: *Circus* is even better than *Baby One More Time*. The tunes are so catchy you'll hum them on the way to work or school. This album is sure to sell well.

B

Too soon ★☆☆☆☆

As if Britney Spears' previous albums weren't bad enough, this one is the pits. Britney's bestselling debut album *Baby One More Time* was promoted so well you felt you had to buy it.

Since then, Britney has made a very public mess of her life, splashed across newspapers all over the world as her marriage fell apart.

Britney's new album, *Circus* proves that she can't sing. The tunes are catchy but the lyrics are **inane**. She sings them as if she has a heavy cold. With luck, this album will be a flop and Britney will finally disappear from the pop world.

Glossary

inane: stupid, empty

How does it work?

- One similarity is that both texts say Britney Spears has appeared in lots of newspapers.

- One difference is that Passage A suggests that Britney's new album will be a success but Passage B suggests it will be a flop.

Here are two reviews of the latest James Bond film. Read them and discuss the questions below with a partner.

A

The latest James Bond film *Quantum of Solace* is very exciting with plenty of action and fast car chases.

The baddie is an evil and nasty looking man who deserves what he gets.

The locations are amazing and there's a good bit of mid-air action around one of them. With so much running, chasing and killing, you have no time to get bored.

Daniel Craig is as cool as ever and he's a great actor. One of the best Bond films ever!

B

The new James Bond film *Quantum of Solace* is sometimes brilliant and thrilling but in the end a big disappointment.

Daniel Craig is even more angry and brutal than he was in the last film. The plot is difficult to follow and though there are plenty of babes, the villains are a bit wet.

Bond jumps and fights his way from one great location to the next but overall the story is so weak that it's hard to care much. If you miss this film, you won't regret it.

- What does each writer think of the film? Do they say you should go and see it?
- Find one point they agree on and one point they disagree on.

Write up your answer, using these prompts to help you:

One similarity between the two reviews is that they both think that...

They disagree over their views about...

Development activity

1 Write two reviews of a film you have seen recently. Mention the story line and write about the characters and the setting. One review needs to make the film sound like it is worth watching and the other review will make people stay at home!

2 **Compare reviews.** Use the internet to find two different reviewers' opinions of the same film, book or TV programme. What are the key similarities and differences?

Check your progress

LEVEL 3	I can understand the main points of the texts
LEVEL 4	I can compare the main points of difference between two texts
LEVEL 5	I can select similarities and differences between two texts and give my opinion

11

This lesson will
● help you to support your ideas using details from the text.

When you are making a point about a text, you need to be able to support your idea with evidence. Every time you make a comment, try to explain your opinion and include relevant detail to back it up.

Getting you thinking

Look at the leaflet below. This has been designed to promote the Slimbridge centre to visitors.

Question: How have the designers of the leaflet tried to make Slimbridge look like an attractive place to visit?

● With a partner, come up with two points you could make.

How does it work?

The next stage in commenting is to include details that support the points you have made.

Have a look at this student's first point:

> The leaflet makes Slimbridge look an attractive place to visit by including some good photographs. These show family members of all ages. They look like they are enjoying the activities as they are smiling.

The student has successfully picked out a design feature used in the leaflet. They have supported their point with detail and explained *why* this makes Slimbridge seem attractive.

something new each season

WWT Slimbridge Wetland Centre

Join us when our ducklings hatch in late spring, flowers bloom and our waders return amidst growth anew.
spring

See willow warblers and spot baby kingfishers fledge from the nest. Spot grass snakes, dragonflies and hares on our Land Rover safaris.
summer

Look out for our migratory birds who return to the reserve each year. See magnificent fungi and stunning sunsets against a backdrop of changing colours.
autumn

Slimbridge transforms into a winter wonderland when our families of Bewick's swans return along with hundreds of thousands of migratory ducks and geese.
winter

« see what's waiting for you

wwt.org.uk/slimbridge

Now you try it **APP**

Here is a leaflet from The London Dungeon. Read through it and then work in pairs to answer the question below.

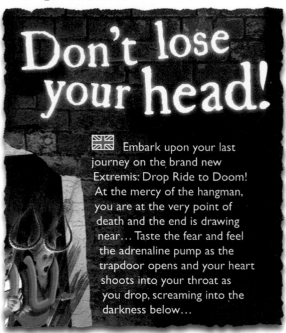

Question: How have the designers of the leaflet tried to make The London Dungeon look like an interesting place to visit?

- In pairs look at the leaflet and come up with two different points to discuss.
- Looking at the leaflet, what has the designer done to make it look interesting? Give two examples.

Glossary

adrenaline: a hormone produced by the body in response to fear and excitement.

Development activity

Design. Your school has decided to update its image with a short leaflet to persuade parents to send their child to the school.

In groups of four draw a mock-up for what the leaflet should look like. Make sure you give details of the attractions your school has to offer.

Ensure you include a range of different design features, such as pictures and headings.

Check your progress		
	LEVEL 3	I can find one example of what the designer has done
	LEVEL 4	I can choose several details from the leaflet and begin to comment on them
	LEVEL 5	I can select appropriate details from the leaflet and comment on them fully

This lesson will
- teach you to select quotations to support your ideas.

When you are writing about a text, you need to find words and phrases from the text that prove your point. These are called quotations.

Remember

It is best to choose a short quotation.

Getting you thinking

Read this opening to a charity brochure. It is trying to persuade you to donate money.

> **Can you honestly think of a way that just £2 a month could do more good, for good?**
>
> Dear Friend
>
> Every 17 seconds, a child in the developing world dies from water related diseases. In around the time it takes you to read this paragraph, someone, somewhere will die. Every day, people in the world's poorest countries have to trust their health and that of their children to drinking water that could kill them. It's a gamble that often carries a high price – seeing children needlessly dying is simply heartbreaking.

Question: How does the writer try to persuade you that dirty water is a serious problem in the developing world?

- With your partner, pick out any words or phrases that suggest this.

Glossary

Developing world is a term used to describe countries where people do not always enjoy a high standard of living

How does it work?

Here is one student's response:

> The writer makes it sound like a serious problem by including details about how many children die. For example, it says, 'every seventeen seconds a child dies'. They also say that because of the dirty water 'children die needlessly'. This makes it sound as if it should not happen.

Each time the student makes a point she picks out a quotation that supports it.

Look at this extract from an RSPCA charity brochure.

Some cruel people still throw animals away as if they were rubbish.

Dear Friend,

I hope that, like me, you care about animals. If so, the thought of puppies and kittens being thrown away like so much rubbish will make you distressed and angry. Yet it happens all the time. If we're lucky and reach them in time, the RSPCA will care for these innocent victims until we can find them loving new homes.

Take Harvey, who's a very affectionate black and white puppy. Yet at just eight weeks old he was **callously** abandoned. One cold night someone stuffed him into a holdall with his five brothers and sisters, and left them outside a pub on a busy road. They could have easily died.

Glossary

sympathy: feeling sorry for someone or something

callously: done without feeling

Complete the answers to the following questions by finding short quotations from the texts.

1 How does the writer make us feel sympathy for badly treated animals?

The writer makes us feel sympathy for badly treated animals by saying that puppies and kittens are '…'.

2 How do most people feel about kittens and puppies being badly treated?

Most people feel '…'.

3 How does the RSPCA care for these animals?

The RSPCA cares by finding them '….'.

4 What was cruelly done to Harvey and his brothers and sisters?

Check your progress

LEVEL 3	I sometimes use quotations from the text
LEVEL 4	I can find quotations to support my ideas
LEVEL 5	I am able to explain the quotations I have chosen

Level Booster

LEVEL 3

- I can pick out basic information from a text
- I can find the main parts of a text
- I can discuss the main parts of a text

LEVEL 4

- I can identify the key pieces of information in a text
- I can select relevant pieces of information from a range of texts
- I can support my ideas with detail from the text
- I can refer to the text itself by picking out quotations

LEVEL 5

- I can select the most relevant pieces of information in a text
- I can read across several texts and pick out the most relevant points
- I am able to select short, relevant and meaningful quotations
- I can make good and accurate points about a text and support them with a quotation and my own explanation

Chapter 2

AF3 Deduce, infer or interpret information, events or ideas from texts

This chapter is going to show you how to

- Make inferences from what you read
- Make sense of information from different points in the text
- Interpret what you read to make deductions about themes, characters and events
- Use skimming and scanning skills to locate information in a text

What's it all about?

Reading between the lines.

This lesson will
● show you how to draw inferences from a text.

When you make inferences from what you read, you look for meanings that are not obvious. This is sometimes called 'reading between the lines'.

Getting you thinking

Read this short paragraph.

> Daisy sat on her own in a chair by the window. The minutes went by slowly but no one talked or spoke to her.

● With a partner, write down everything we find out about Daisy.

How does it work?

We are told directly that a woman named Daisy is alone. She doesn't have a conversation with anyone.

But we could also make some **inferences** about *why* Daisy is alone. We could **infer** (work out) that she is lonely or unpopular or wants company or has nothing to do. None of these things are said for certain, but they are **suggested** by the text.

Now you try it

Here is the opening to an article from *The Daily Mirror* (9 October 2008).

Love thy neighbour

JULIE McIlroy had spent months scouring the world for love on a dating website but just couldn't find a fella.

She finally spotted a picture of someone she fancied and began chatting to Allan Donnelly online.

The teacher, 46, then made an extraordinary discovery – they lived in the **SAME** street.

Stunned by the amazing coincidence, they simply walked out of their homes to meet each other for the first time.

Read the extract and try to answer this question:

○ What do we learn from the article about love?

Start…

I think the article is saying that…

I also think it suggests that love can happen…

Development activity

Now read the rest of the article.

> Now the couple plan to marry next year. Mum of three Julie said yesterday: 'I was totally stunned. It just goes to show you never know where you will find love.'
>
> 'The dating site could've put me in touch with someone anywhere in the world. Well, they say 'Love thy neighbour, don't they?'
>
> Dad of two, Allan, 53, added with a smile. 'It was my lucky day. We're perfect together.'

Discuss which of the following statements you think would be reasonable conclusions to draw from the article as a whole:

a You will probably find someone you love in your street

b A dating website is a good way to meet your perfect partner

c People called Julie and Allan usually fall in love.

d Luck plays a big part in finding happiness.

This lesson will
- help you to understand what is happening in different parts of a newspaper article.

Your understanding of a text can change as you read through it. As you consider information at different points, you find out different things. For example, a newspaper headline provides clues about the article that follows. But you'll need to read on to find out the whole story.

Getting you thinking

Here is the headline from a report in the *Daily Mail* (8 October 2008):

> **High School Musical mania hits Britain as heart-throb Zac meets thousands of adoring fans**

- What do you think the article is going to be about, based on the headline?

How does it work?

You could say:

> We are told the name of the film that the article is going to be about and of its star. We are also told about 'mania' and 'heart-throb' Zac's 'adoring fans'. These three things suggest the article will be about Zac's popularity with his fans, who love him.

Now you try it

Read on and ask yourself – is this *all* the article is about?

He arrived with a smile that revealed more gleaming teeth than it seemed possible to fit in one mouth. Hair swept back in a flowing quiff, his eyes flashed bright blue in the grey evening light. Nothing in a teenage girl's dreams could have matched the moment they were able to see their Zac Efron in the flesh.

The star of High School Musical arrived to scenes of **hysteria**. Or, rather, the world of under-16 teenyboppers, some of whom queued in the drizzle for up to 14 hours to see their heart-throb.

Screaming girls aged from four upwards cheered their young idol, threw flowers and messages of love. One even proposed marriage.

Glossary

hysteria: over-excitement

- Write down one new thing we learn from the article about Zac Efron.
- Write down one new thing we learn from the article about his fans.
- Why do you think the headline doesn't tell us all this information?

Development activity

In small groups, look at this set of facts. It was included with the article about Zac's arrival at the premiere of *High School Musical 3*.

Discuss:

- Why you think these facts have been included.
- What the facts tell us. Choose the best answer (or answers) from the list below.

  a *High School Musical 3* is going to be very successful

  b People aren't that interested in Zac Efron.

  c The *High School Musical* films are very popular.

  d *High School Musical 3* is going to be a flop.

BY NUMBERS

£500,000
advance UK ticket sales for High School Musical 3, a new record

670
spin-off products – soon to include the High School Musical 3 video game to be in shops in time for Christmas

250 million
viewers worldwide have seen the original High School Musical film, which came out in 2006

Check your progress

LEVEL 3 I can recognise different parts of a text

LEVEL 4 I can tell you about the different parts of a text

LEVEL 5 I can comment in detail on different parts of a text and their purpose

3 Interpret what you read to make deductions about themes, characters and events (Part 1)

This lesson will
- help you to understand themes and character
- help you to make deductions about themes and character.

When we 'interpret' what happens in a text, we make a judgement about what is happening. We think about what someone is like (their **character**), why something happened (the **events**) and what the point of the story might be (the **themes**).

Getting you thinking

Look at the cover and **blurb** for this novel, *In the Middle of the Night* by Robert Cormier.

Do not pick up the phone. Let your mother or me answer it. If it's for you, I will hand it over. Alone in the house, you do not answer.

The phone calls come every year, waking Denny up in the middle of the night. Every year, Denny's father calmly answers. He never speaks. He simply listens. But this year it's different. It's twenty-five years since the fire, the terrible tragedy for which Denny's father bears the blame. The tragedy which triggered these calls, year in, year out.

This year, Denny has had enough. This year, he will pick up the phone – and face the consequences.

Discuss with the person next to you:
- What do you think the story (the **events**) might be about?
- What or who do you think the main characters might be?
- What themes do you think might be important in the novel?

Glossary

blurb: a short summary or taster of the story, which appears on the back cover of a book

How does it work?

Here is one student's answer to the third question:

> Judging by the blurb, a theme of the novel might be guilt as it says that Denny's father blames himself.

Notice that the answer makes a connection between the **evidence** (what it says in the blurb) and the **interpretation** (what the student *thinks*).

Now you try it

Look at the opening paragraph of the novel.

Chapter 1

The first call usually came some time in October, a week or two before the anniversary. This, however, was early September. In the final hours of a **lingering** heat wave. Fans turned lazily in the bedroom windows, fans that did not blur the sound of the telephone, **incessant** and **insistent**. Please make it a wrong number, he prayed.

Discuss:
- What are we told in this extract?
- How would you interpret the *mood* of the writing?
- Does it match the blurb?

Glossary

lingering: hanging around and not going away

incessant: non-stop and never-ending

insistent: firm and not giving up

Development activity

Look at the two sample answers below. Explain which one you think is best and why.

1 We are told about the phone call and the nice hot weather. The extract seems happy and joyful because it's during hot weather which people like. It doesn't match the blurb which seemed frightening.

2 It starts with 'The first call' and later mentions the constant ringing of the telephone which won't go away. It raises questions in our mind: who is on the phone? Why are they phoning? This adds to the theme of mystery. The extract links well to the mood of the blurb which was mysterious and threatening, too.

Check your progress

LEVEL 3 I can see that the example answers are different

LEVEL 4 I can understand which example answer is better

LEVEL 5 I can comment in detail on which answer is better, providing evidence for my ideas

This lesson will
● help you to make deductions about characters and events.

We have already made some interpretations about Denny from what we have read:

● He wants answers to his questions.
● He is prepared to face whatever might happen.
● He is frightened.

Getting you thinking

In the following extract, taken from later in the novel, Denny is at school.

> Denny didn't want any individual attention, however. Just the opposite: he wanted to blend in and not call attention to himself. He was a shadow without **substance**, **gliding** through his hours in the corridors and classrooms like a ghost. He did not volunteer answers.

● What do you learn about him here?

Glossary

substance: weight
gliding: moving easily or smoothly

How does it work?

We can work out what Denny is *like* (his **character**) by looking at:

1 How he behaves and what he does

   …gliding through his hours in the corridors and classrooms like a ghost.
   He did not volunteer answers.

2 What he says (about himself)

   …he wanted to blend in and not call attention to himself.

3 Any direct descriptions by the writer

   He was a shadow without substance…

Now you try it

From these descriptions, can you work out what Denny is like at this point in the novel? Which of these seems the best description of him?

a Denny is a naturally shy, but happy boy.

b Denny is confident and outgoing.

c Denny is withdrawn and keen to keep things to himself.

Once you have decided, write one sentence explaining your choice.

I think Denny is... because...

Development activity

Finally, what about the **events** in the story?

Read the following extract. Your teacher will explain what has happened in the story so far.

> The newspaper trembled in his hands. He was alone in the house. He heard the thump of the paper thrown against the back door by the kid who delivered it every day. He brought it into the house, **averting** his eyes from the front page and the headlines, then told himself that he could not go through life avoiding newspapers. Glancing **tentatively** at the front page, was relieved to find no story about the Globe. Same with page two.

Glossary

averting his eyes: looking away

tentatively: nervously

Discuss with a partner:

- How can we tell from reading this extract that the newspaper – and what might be in it – is important?

Think about...

The way Denny reacts to the arrival of the paper

The words used to describe his actions.

Check your progress

LEVEL 3	I can understand the extract
LEVEL 4	I can work out what is happening and how the character might be feeling
LEVEL 5	I can write in detail about the character and events, using evidence from the text

This lesson will
- show you how to use skimming and scanning techniques.

When reading a text, it is important to be able to find specific pieces of information. Two techniques called skimming and scanning will help you do this.

Skimming: looking at a text quickly to get a general idea of its contents.
Scanning: looking at a text for specific bits of information.

Getting you thinking

Read this extract from an article about Tiger Woods:

Tiger Woods wins the US Masters again

When Tiger won the US Masters in 1997, he was only twenty-one years old. In winning, he broke lots of records. He won the title by 12 strokes, which was the biggest ever victory at the US Open. He also became the youngest champion in sixty-one years.

In 2000, Tiger won the US Open by an amazing 15 stroke margin. He has won the US Open three times so far. Tiger is the youngest ever player to achieve the number one world ranking.

- First, 'skim' the text to find out what it is about.

  You might say:

  By skimming through the text, I have worked out that the article is about Tiger Woods. It's about his victories on the golf course and all the tournaments he has won.

- You are now going to 'scan' the text and look for specific pieces of information.

  1 At what age did Tiger Woods first win the US Masters?

  2 How many strokes did he win the US Open by in 2000?

  3 How many times has Tiger Woods won the US Open?

Now you try it

Here is the **blurb** for a book called *The Trap* by John Smelcer. It is a book for teenagers.

> **It was getting colder. Johnny pulled the fur-lined hood of his parka over his head and walked toward his own cabin with the sound of snow crunching beneath his boots. 'He should be back tomorrow,' he thought, as a star raced across the sky just below the North Star. 'He should be back tomorrow for sure.'**
>
> Johnny's grandfather has taken far too much time to check his trap lines in the Alaskan snow. The old man is proud and stubborn, and determined to be as independent as ever. But Johnny is right to worry – his grandfather has caught his foot in his own trap. Wolves, plummeting temperatures and sheer hunger all menace him. Does he have enough wilderness craft, strength and survival instinct to stay alive? Will Johnny find him in time?

'An unforgettable story. Brilliant!'
RAY BRADBURY

THE TRAP

JOHN SMELCER

Work in pairs to **skim** through the blurb. Write down two things you learn about the story and where is it set.

Development activity

Now, **scan** the text and answer the following questions.

1 What is Johnny wearing?

2 What has happened to his grandfather

3 What three things threaten his grandfather?

Now you've skimmed and scanned the blurb, is this a book you would like to read yourself? Why or why not?

Check your progress

LEVEL 3	I can find simple pieces of information from the text
LEVEL 4	I can use skimming and scanning to find the information I need
LEVEL 5	I can write detailed responses to the questions on the text

Level Booster

LEVEL 3

- I can understand most things I read
- I can pick up on specific points in texts
- I can make simple responses to texts

LEVEL 4

- I can make inferences from texts that I read
- I can make sense of information from different points in texts
- I can make deductions about themes, characters and events
- I can use skimming and scanning skills when looking for information in a text

LEVEL 5

- I can make inferences from more complicated texts
- I can select essential ideas at different points in texts
- I can identify key points about themes, characters and events and write about these points
- I can use quotations from texts in my writing to support my own views and explain them

Chapter 3

AF4 Identify and comment on the structure and organisation of texts

This chapter is going to show you how to

- Identify whether a text is put together in a structured and organised way
- Recognise and understand the organisation of different texts
- Understand the use of headings and bullet points
- Understand the structure of stories
- Comment on the form of a poem.

What's it all about?

Looking at structure and layout.

Identify whether a text is put together in a structured and organised way

This lesson will

● help you to understand whether a text is organised.

Knowing whether something you are reading is well constructed will help you to discuss the text and the writer's choices. It will also help you with your own writing.

Getting you thinking

Your friend has written this account of a trip to Windsor Castle. He's asked you for your opinion on the quality of his writing:

When we got there it was cold and crowded. We got on the bus at eight thirty and it took us half an hour to arrive. Mrs Pinell met us outside reception. I got up at seven this morning and had breakfast. All week I looked forward to it. Last week I found out that my class was going to Windsor Castle. Some people weren't interested in going but I was very excited as I had never been there before, so I got my mum to make sure she paid straight away. We got back to school at two o'clock. Windsor Castle was very busy. There must have been two or three other schools there. We looked round the grounds and visited the chapel. The castle is a lot bigger than it looks and there is a doll's house if you like that sort of thing. I had a good time, and I recommend it to everyone.

● What would you say to him?

How does it work?

You probably

- understood the things your friend did
- got the idea that he enjoyed the trip
- found parts of it difficult to follow.

This is because your friend needs to **organise his ideas** better and **structure his paragraph**.

The problem is that all the events of the story seem to be mixed up. He hasn't thought about the **order of his sentences**.

He needs to go back and think about *what* happened *when* (what we call the **chronology** of events) and write the sentences in that order.

> ### Glossary
>
> **chronology:** a record of events in the order of when they occurred

Now you try it

Look back at what your friend wrote. Number each sentence in what you think should be the correct order. For example,

> *1 Last week I found out that...*

Now decide whether there are any unnecessary sentences and remove them. Then, rewrite the paragraph.

Development activity

The paragraph can still be improved.

1 Discuss with your partner how you could

- add some words or sentences to make the paragraph flow better. (For example, where could you add words such as *then*, *later* or *next*?)
- divide the paragraph. (For example, could you turn this into *two paragraphs* showing when there is a change in time or scene?)

Check your progress

LEVEL 3	I understand what structure and organisation mean
LEVEL 4	I can recognise when a text is organised and structured
LEVEL 5	I can discuss a few ways in which a text is organised and structured

This lesson will
- help you to understand the layouts of different texts.

Each text has its own particular organisation. For example, an email doesn't usually *look* like a large newspaper! Understanding how different texts are organised will help you to decide what their **purposes** are and who they are aimed at (their **audience**).

Getting you thinking

Match the images to the types of texts listed below.

Notice about what to do in case of a fire
Newspaper article
Encyclopaedia page

Now match the following organisational features to the types of text (remember *some* of these may be relevant to more than one text):

Columns
Pictures and diagrams
Photos
Bullet points

Paragraphs
Alphabetical order
Headings
Headlines

How does it work?

Look at how you might write about the structure and organisation of *one* of these texts. Notice how the writer talks about the text's **purpose** and **audience**:

The fire notice is made up of symbols, headings and instructions written in quick and easy to understand bullet points. It is aimed at people facing an emergency situation – a fire. For this reason, the notice needs to be clear and easy to follow.

Now you try it APP

Write a paragraph about how this webpage is organised. You might want to include comments about:

- the importance of being able to find what you want
- links to other pages
- headings or headlines
- menus
- the use of images and video clips.

Start…

The webpage is organised in the following way. It uses…

Continue…

The purpose of the webpage is to give the reader…

BBC   Low graphics   Help   Search   Explore the BBC

SPORT   THE OLYMPIC BROADCASTER   ▶ Watch Sport news bulletin

Football
Formula One
Olympics
Cricket
Rugby Union
Rugby League
Tennis
Golf
Athletics
Cycling
Motorsport
Boxing
Snooker
Horse Racing
Disability Sport
Other sport...
Sports Personality
Video and Audio
TV/Radio Schedule
Scores & Fixtures
606

Page last updated at 15:48 GMT, Wednesday, 11 March 2009   Sport Feeds

HORSE RACING: Master Minded defends the Queen Mother Champion Chase from Well Chief at Cheltenham. More soo

I can take any booing - Beckham

David Beckham tells BBC Sport he can handle any hostility from LA Galaxy fans when he eventually returns to the United States to continue his MLS career.

› Beckham will be booed, says Lalas
› Beckham injures ankle in training

CLICK TO PLAY

RUGBY UNION
England change three for France
◀ Johnson wants more discipline
› Chabal switches to flanker

HORSE RACING
Live text - Cheltenham Festiva
◀ Live - Cheltenham commentary
› Nicholls pair top Gold Cup field
› Cheltenham day two photos

FOOTBALL
Ferguson wary of Mourinho effect
▶ Ferguson expects tough tie
▶ Game all about pressure - Mourinho
› Man Utd v Inter Milan team news

Internet

Development activity

Which of the following organisational features would you normally find in a recipe?

Photos	*Paragraphs*
Lists	*A clear order of events*
Rhyme	*Big headlines*

Check your progress

LEVEL 3 I can spot different types of texts

LEVEL 4 I can recognise different types of texts and comment on their organisation

LEVEL 5 I can recognise the type or genre of a text and understand reader expectations

Understand the use of headings and bullet points

This lesson will
- help you to understand how and why bullet points and headings are used.

Knowing how headings and bullet points are used in leaflets and other information texts will help you to understand and comment on them.

Getting you thinking

Look at the following leaflet for *Laser Zone* in Scarborough.

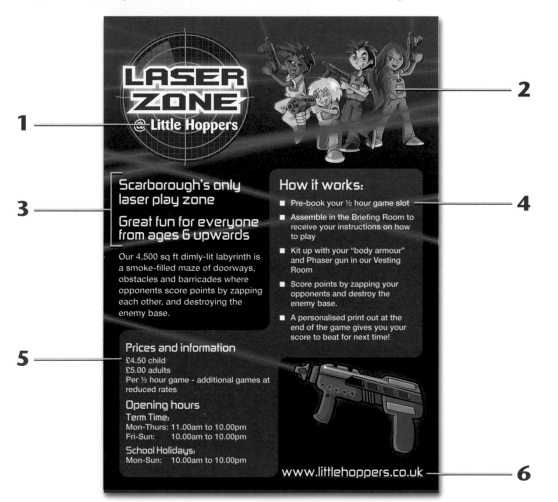

- Can you copy out the numbers and write down what each one is pointing to?
- What do the headings tell us?
- How do the bullet points help to give us information about Laser Zone?

Now you try it

Look again at the leaflet. This time think about its **design** (how it looks).

- What comments could you make about the background to the heading LASER ZONE?
- Why do you think there are streaks of red across the leaflet?

Development activity (APP)

Look at this leaflet from the visitor attraction, *The Tales of Robin Hood*.

- How do the headings and bullet points help us to know what the leaflet is about?
- Think about the colours and pictures in the leaflet. Why might these have been chosen?

Write a paragraph about the way the leaflet has been organised, commenting on the devices used, including headings and bullet points.

Use this frame if you need to:

Headings and bullet points have been used to...

The leaflet uses colour to...

The pictures chosen are...

Another thing that catches the reader's eye is ...

THE TALES OF ROBIN HOOD

During your visit.....

- You will travel back in time on our Adventure Ride
- Show your true allegiance to Robin with our interactive Silver Arrow Quiz
- Join the outlaws for Archery Practice (small charge payable)
- Take part in an Activity Workshop (please ring for details of educational packages)
- Fact or Fantasy? Hear the evidence in our film show and make up your own mind.
- Learn about the medieval art of Falconry (in the centre or Castle Grounds - bookable in advance)

Check your progress

LEVEL 3	I understand that bullet points can be used in some texts
LEVEL 4	I can tell you about how headings and bullet points are used in leaflets
LEVEL 5	I can discuss the effect of presentational devices on readers

4 Understand the structure of stories

This lesson will

● help you to understand how stories are put together.

Understanding how stories are structured will help you to follow them… and enjoy them! You will also be able to discuss how the writer has organised the story to make it exciting. To achieve a Level 4 you need to be able to comment on some basic parts of story structure.

Getting you thinking

Most stories are organised in the following way:

Stage of the story	What could this mean?
Stories *begin* with some sort of *introduction*.	We might meet the main character, or be told about the setting – where the story starts.
They *develop* because of some sort of problem or complication.	The main character might learn some bad news or something might happen, which he or she has to respond to (for example, solve a mystery).
They come to a *key moment*.	Events build up, reaching a key, dramatic moment when, for example, the main character faces his or her problem or situation and deals with it.
They end with *resolution* – the situation is completed and any problems are sorted out.	After the key moment, we might learn what happens to the characters next. Sometimes the background to why things happened is revealed.

Look at the following version of a well-known story.
It is called 'The Pardoner's Tale'.

● When you have heard the story read aloud, look back at the table. Point to the paragraphs in 'The Pardoner's Tale' that you think cover the Introduction stage.

● Then, discuss what you find out, and who is introduced.

Three young men were sitting playing cards in a tavern, when they heard a ringing outside. Someone must have died. Out of curiosity the eldest called out to a boy, 'Boy, who's dead?'

He replied, 'Well, sir, he used to be a friend of yours – killed last night by a local fellow, known round here as Death. Knifed him right through the heart.'

The young men being drunk and foolish said, 'We'll sort him out. Who the hell does he think he is?! We'll search high and low till we find him.'

Despite the warnings from the publican the three young men set off in the direction of the village where Death had last been seen.

They'd hardly gone half a mile when they came across a weak-looking, old man. The young men made fun of him and were rude to him. 'Get out of our way, old man!' they jeered. 'Why are you still alive?'

'Because Death hasn't taken me yet,' he replied. 'But why are you so rude?' he said as he passed by them. Before he could go the hooligans grabbed him and asked him how he knew Death and where they could find him.

'Well,' said the old man, 'if you're looking for Death you'll find him over there – along that path and near that tree.' He pointed ahead of him and bid them goodbye. The men didn't even thank him. They just rushed off in search of Death.

When they came to the tree they saw a sack full of gold and all thoughts of Death disappeared from their minds.

'Look at this,' said the ringleader. 'It's ours now – we're rich. Finders keepers!'

'Mm,' he pondered. 'We need to move it back to our place but we should do it at night. Don't want people thinking we are thieves, do we?'

'Yes, but we need food and drink to keep us going till then,' said one of the others.

The leader picked three straws from the ground and continued, 'Whoever gets the short straw goes back to town to get drink and food. The others stand guard over the loot.'

The men agreed and so the youngest who'd drawn the short straw headed off to town. When he was out of sight the leader, who was the wickedest, said 'Wouldn't it be good to share the money just between the two of us?'

He told the other of his plan to kill the youngest man when he returned.

Meanwhile the youngest man was plotting himself. He bought poison and put it into the wine which he carried back to the two others. When he got to them they attacked him just as they had planned. Then they sat down to celebrate and in drinking the wine they too died.

In the end, it seems that the three young men found Death after all!

Now you try it

Copy and complete the grid below, based on the Tale.
The first part has been done for you.

Stage	What we are told
Introduction	Three young men go in search of 'Death'
Development (complication?)	
Key moment	
Ending (resolution)	

Development activity

Then turn the grid into a short commentary on the structure of the tale. Use this frame if you wish:

I think in the introduction to the tale, we are told about...

The story then develops when...

The key moment is the point when...

It ends with...

Check your progress

LEVEL 3	I know a story has a beginning, middle and end
LEVEL 4	I can comment on the structure of a story
LEVEL 5	I can discuss different ways that stories can be structured

5 Comment on the form of a poem

> **This lesson will**
> ● help you to understand how poems are put together.

The form of a poem is its shape (how it looks on the page), its rhythm and its rhyme (when it has one). Being able to comment on the form of a poem will help you to understand the effect it has on the reader.

Getting you thinking

There are a number of different forms that poems can take.

Here is one. Hear it read aloud first and then try to answer the questions below.

> I always eat peas with honey
> I've done it all my life,
> They do taste kind of funny,
> But it keeps them on the knife!
>
> Anon

● Do you notice any words that rhyme?
● Does the poem have a strong rhythm?
● How does the form fit the poem's meaning, if at all?

How does it work?

Here is a short commentary on the poem's form:

The poem has a regular rhythm, with alternate rhyming lines (honey/funny; life/knife). It is short – only four lines long. The rhyme and regular rhythm give it a sing-song feel, like a funny playground chant.

The key words for commenting on form here are:

regular (it has a repeating pattern)

alternate (= every other line)

line (how a poem is organised)

rhythm (the sound and beat of the poem)

like a... playground chant (links the poem to another type of rhyme).

Now you try it

Locking Up

A frail old woman lived by herself
As jittery as a mouse.
When darkness fell she locked all locks
In her rickety rambling house.

She bolted bolts and hooked all hooks
(No window left unshut):
She checked and rechecked twenty times
To be quite certain … But

What was that? Close to her ear
A whisper faint and thin,
Nobody there, but a **phantom** voice:
'Now we're both locked in.'

Ian Serraillier

Glossary

phantom: ghostly

Hear the poem read aloud. Then, with a partner, discuss:

1 What is the mood of the poem?

2 Does the mood of the poem change at all? If so, where?

3 How do you think the old woman feels about living alone?

4 How many verses are there?

5 Do you notice any rhymes or repeated words?

Development activity APP

Now try writing a paragraph where you make one or two comments about the poem's *form* and how it fits the poem's *meaning*, or *mood*.

For example,

> The poem has lots of …
> This helps to create a … mood.
> I think the old woman feels …
> The end of the poem is surprising because …

Check your progress

LEVEL 3	I understand that poems take different forms
LEVEL 4	I can tell you about a poem's form
LEVEL 5	I can comment in detail on how a poem's form relates to its meaning

Level Booster

LEVEL 3

- I can understand what structure and organisation mean
- I can tell if sentences make sense
- I can tell if a story makes sense
- I understand that bullet points can be used in some texts

LEVEL 4

- I can recognise when a text is organised and structured
- I can recognise and understand different types of texts and their organisation
- I can understand a sequence of events in a story: introduction, development, key moment and ending
- I can tell you about headings and bullet points
- I can tell you about the form of a poem

LEVEL 5

- I can recognise the genre of a text and understand reader expectations
- I can identify structural features in a text
- I can understand how different texts are structured
- I can discuss the effect of presentational devices on readers
- I can understand why writers choose different forms for poems

Chapter 4

AF5 Explain and comment on writer's use of language, including grammatical and literary features at word and sentence level

This chapter is going to show you how to

- Comment on similes
- Understand writers' word choices
- Understand how writers use sentences
- Understand how writers use dialogue
- Identify different tenses

What's it all about?

Explain how writers use words and sentences.

Comment on similes

This lesson will
- help you to identify similes
- help you to explain how they make description come alive.

A simile is an **image** – a **word picture**. In similes, writers compare what they are describing with something similar.

To **comment** on similes, you must first identify them. Then you need to say how they fit the thing described.

Getting you thinking

Read this paragraph aloud together.

A

> The factory chimneys smoked like fat cigars. Around them lay rows of terraced houses like lines of dominoes. In the morning the workers were drawn from these houses to the factory, like iron filings dragged towards a magnet. In the evening they returned, young men puffed up like full-blown sails, old men bent like thorn trees on a windy hillside, girls gossiping like flights of starlings.

- The similes in this example all use 'like'. Can you spot them? There are six.

How does it work?

Once you have found a simile, the next stage in commenting is to try to imagine or picture what is being described.

Look again at Example A. Imagine the rows of houses 'like lines of dominoes'.

Next, ask yourself *how* the two things are similar. Why is the author comparing them?

The houses are like dominoes because –
- they are all in a row
- they all look the same
- they are **rectangular**.

Glossary

rectangular: shaped like a rectangle

To comment on the simile, you might say:

> The writer compares the houses to lines of dominoes
> because they are all in a row and look the same.
> The houses are rectangular, like dominoes. It makes
> the houses sound small and squashed together.

Now you try it

Read the following paragraph. Here the similes all use 'as'.

B

> At Christmas, the snow lay thick as icing on a
> wedding cake, cold as marble, white as a bridal gown.
> The children's cheeks glowed red as coals, their noses
> dripped as regularly as a leaky tap, their voices rose
> higher than the angels on All Saints Church.

1 Look at the first simile: 'the snow lay thick *as icing on a wedding cake*'.
How else might snow be like wedding cake icing?

2 Find another simile using 'as' and write it down.
 ○ What two things are being compared?
 ○ Why do you think they are being compared?
 ○ What picture does this create in your head?

Development activity

Example A could continue:

> But up on the hillside was their common destination,
> the graveyard of All Saints Church, its gravestones
> standing like rows of crooked teeth.

1 Copy out the phrase containing the simile in this sentence.
2 Comment on the way it fits what it describes (gravestones).
3 Think up another simile that could be used for the gravestones.
4 In groups, think of different similes to replace all those in Example A.
Agree on the best ones. Then rewrite the passage using them.

Check your progress

LEVEL 3 I can identify similes

LEVEL 4 I can explain what similes mean

LEVEL 5 I can explain how well similes fit what they describe

This lesson will
- help you to understand and explain why a writer chooses certain words.

Writers think very carefully about what words to use. Your job is to understand *why* the writer has chosen these words – how they affect the text's meaning.

Getting you thinking

Peer and Hilde are finding their way along a passage deep inside the mountain stronghold of the trolls – Troll Fell.

Peer pushed in front. 'All right! I'll go first.' He had to keep moving. When he stood still, he felt the whole demanding weight of Troll Fell bearing down on his shoulders. 'Look! Keep near the wall, like this, and – ah!'

His foot slipped on the wet stone lip. In panic, he snatched at the rocks. One hand curled over a sharp rim and he hung by an arm, kicking, poised over the drop. The water drummed on his back. He heard Hilde scream; then her hand bit into his **flailing** wrist and hauled. The rock edge ground into his midriff. He dragged his knee up and over, and clawed himself further up the slippery shelf.

Katherine Langrish, *Troll Fell*

Glossary

flailing: slipping

- Can you find three verbs (doing words) that bring the scene to life, showing us what Peer or Hilde did, and how it felt?

Now you try it

The table below shows some other words and phrases that the writer could have chosen.

With a partner, decide whether the writer's choices are stronger.

If so, explain why.

Author's choice	Alternative
scream	cry out
bit into his flailing wrist	grabbed his waving wrist
hauled	pulled
ground into his midriff	poked him in the tummy
dragged	pulled
clawed himself further	climbed

Development activity

In groups, take it in turns to read out these letter extracts. Then try to answer the questions below.

Letter 1

> I am cross about the groups of youngsters who stand outside my house. These unemployed young people make local residents nervous. They joke as they pass, drop litter on the pavement, and write in bright colours on the wall. They drink Coca Cola and play loud music on their portable sound systems.

Letter 2

> I am furious about the gangs of youths who hang about outside my house. These workshy yobs terrorise local residents. They hurl taunts as they pass, toss rubbish on the pavement, and scrawl graffiti in **garish** colours on the wall. They swill Coca Cola and deafen everyone with the appalling racket of their 'ghetto blasters'.

- Spot the differences and discuss how they change the meaning of the letter.
- Which letter makes the most impact? Why?

Glossary

garish: very bright or loud

This lesson will
- help you to identify different types of sentence
- help you to explain their effects.

Writers can use short, simple sentences or longer, more complex ones. You need to notice the different types of sentence a writer uses and talk about their effect.

Getting you thinking

In this extract, Harry has been picked on by a gang of other boys. He has defended himself and managed to hurt their leader.

Remember

When looking at sentences, ask yourself what the writer's *purpose* is in writing this part of the story.

> They picked up their leader, but he kept doubling up with pain. When he could finally stand unaided, he said, 'I'll stay here an' watch him. You fetch the rest of the lads.'
>
> Eager to do his bidding, they fled and soon vanished over the sandhills.
>
> Harry knew he was in a jam. The leader was still there. If Harry made off and tried to hide, the leader would follow him, and summon up his returning gang from the top of the nearest sand-dune… The leader had to be fixed.
>
> He walked towards him. The leader tried to back off. But he was still in pain. Harry caught up with him easily as he tried to scrabble to safety up the side of the sand-dune.
>
> Harry took careful aim, and hit the leader on the ankle with the curving length of wood. With all his force. It was the only way.
>
> Robert Westall, *The Kingdom by the Sea*

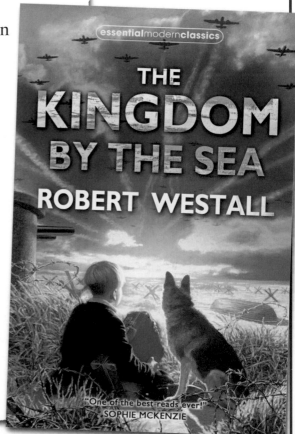

essentialmodernclassics

THE KINGDOM BY THE SEA

ROBERT WESTALL

"One of the best reads ever!"
SOPHIE MCKENZIE

- What do you notice about the length of sentences used in this passage?

Now you try it

1 Look again at the last two paragraphs. With a partner, discuss which sentences create tension and suspense, and why.

2 Rewrite the last paragraph adding whatever words you need to turn it into a single sentence. Read it out. How has the effect changed?

Development activity

Hear the following story opening read aloud and then re-read it yourself.

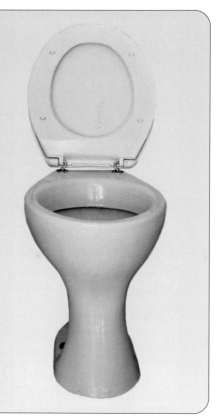

> If you're ready, let's begin. If this was a made-up story, it would begin at night, with a storm blowing and owls hooting and rattling noises under the bed. But this is a real story, so I have to begin where it really started.
>
> It started in a toilet.
>
> Darren Shan, *Cirque du Freak*

- With a partner, talk about the different sentence lengths you notice in the passage.

- Then, write two sentences explaining what you think is the effect of the final short sentence on the reader.

This lesson will
● help you to understand and explain how writers use dialogue to bring a story to life.

Dialogue means characters' conversation in a novel or story, together with the words and phrases telling us who is speaking and how they speak. Dialogue brings a story to life and moves it on. It can also tell us about the characters.

Getting you thinking

Fax and Walkman corner Maisie Malin at break. These are not the boys' school names and this is not school business.

> 'Is it right what we heard?' goes Walkman. His hand on the wall keeps her **corralled**. She peers past his shoulder seeking help she knows won't come.
>
> 'Dunno. Depends what you heard, dunnit?'
>
> The other boy snickers. 'We heard you're starting with the pickles, kiddo. Tonight.'
>
> Maisie nods. 'It's right then.'
>
> 'Who got you on?'
>
> 'My auntie. She's a line supervisor.'
>
> 'She could be the queen of frigging sheba,' murmurs Walkman, 'you work, you tell us. You know that.'
>
> 'Yes, and I know why as well. Why should I give you ten per cent of my wages for nothing?'
>
> Fax snorts. 'Why? Because that's the way things work. Always have, always will. You get push protection.'
>
> 'Oh I know, Push protects me from push. I've seen all those gangster movies too,' Maisie sneers. 'You don't impress me with your daft nickname. Fax! Fix'd be nearer the mark for someone like you. And as for you' – she turns to Longstaff – 'I see you as Dorkman rather than Walkman.'
>
> 'Oh, Maisie,' Walkman shakes his head. 'You aren't half going to wish you hadn't said that.'
>
> Robert Swindells, *Dosh*

Top tips

Writers don't always name the speaker. But you should be able to work out who is speaking because there is a new paragraph for a change of speaker.

Glossary

corralled: trapped

● Do you think Maisie sounds brave or like a frightened coward?

Now you try it

A few days later, Maisie is attacked by two boys wearing masks. They steal her expensive trainers. The following day Walkman (Malcome Longstaffe) confronts her.

'Whoops-a-daisy, Maisie.'

He grins like a wolf. 'I *told* you you'd have to watch your steps from now on, didn't I?'

Maisie draws back. 'What do you want?' Kids are passing but none of them looks at Longstaffe or Maisie. Push business is Push business.

'Me? I don't want *anything*, Maisie, unless there's something you'd like to give me. Is there?'

'I know it was you last night. You and Barraclough. What you done with my trainers?'

'Sorry?'

'Don't pretend you don't know what I'm on about. Cardigan Street. The masks.'

- Discuss with a partner what you learn about each character here, commenting on (a) what they say and (b) how they say it.

Check your progress	LEVEL 3	I understand what dialogue is
	LEVEL 4	I can explain what dialogue tells us about the different characters
	LEVEL 5	I can comment on how dialogue tells us about relationships between characters

This lesson will
- help you to identify different tenses
- show you how they are used.

Verbs (doing or being words) come in different tenses. The tense is the particular form of the verb that shows when something is happening:

past (I went ...)   present (I go ...)   or future (I will go ...)

Stories tend to be told in the past tense. But the present tense is useful for creating special effects.

Remember

Use the present tense to write about novels, poems and plays: 'Michael *finds* Skellig in the garage.'

Getting you thinking

Look at these examples.

1 Past tense

They hurried into their swimming things, rubbing their arms against the chilly wind.
　　'OK. Last one in's a wimp!' challenged Amir.
　　'You said it,' yelled Nina, racing ahead of him.
　　As they reached the water's edge, the pair were neck and neck.
　　'Wait!' shouted Amir in a tone of alarm. 'Isn't that a fin sticking out of the water?'

2 Present tense

At last she hears Dad's snores. She flicks on the torch – the bedside light is too risky – swings her feet to the floor, and fumbles into her dressing gown. The door creaks and she holds her breath. Halfway down the stairs she hears a sound in the garden, a crunch of gravel. She freezes. Is it him?

3 Future tense

Most parts of Britain will have rain at first. Luckily the sun will chase away those rain clouds by midday, and the afternoon will be mostly dry. Temperatures will reach 24 degrees centigrade in parts, so you'll need your sun-cream.

- Why do you think the writer of the second extract chose to write in the present tense? Discuss with a partner.

How does it work?

The present tense is often used to create suspense: to make the reader feel as if they are there with the character.

The future tense is used in forecasts, predictions and promises.

Now you try it

Rewrite Passage 2 opposite from the present tense into the past tense.

1 Copy out the passage. Each time you come to a **verb** (a doing or being word), you will need to change it from the **present tense** (hears, flicks) to the **past tense** (heard, flicked).

Remember, most verbs in the past tense end in '-ed'.

2 Then read your new version to your partner and discuss the effect of this change.

Development activity

1 What tense is the passage below in?

> I look at Alfie and Alfie looks at me. We're both thinking the same thing. The soldiers are getting closer every second. I can hear the clank of an armoured car and orders shouted hoarsely above its din. There's no way forward. Behind us there are two choices: a winding path with no cover, where they'd pick us off like ducks in a shooting range, or a hundred foot drop into the deep blue sea.
>
> 'Can you swim?' I ask.

Remember

Look out for any changes of tense in what you are reading. Has the writer done this to create a special effect?

2 Write at least one more paragraph continuing the story in this tense.

Check your progress

LEVEL 3	I understand what tenses are
LEVEL 4	I can identify the three main tenses
LEVEL 5	I can comment on a writer's choice of tense

Level Booster

LEVEL 3

- I understand what a simile is
- I can see why some word choices are better than others
- I can identify what makes a sentence
- I can tell when characters are speaking
- I can identify present, past and future tenses

LEVEL 4

- I can pick out similes and talk about them
- I understand that a writer's word choices affect the text's meaning
- I can comment on how writers vary sentence length
- I understand how writers use dialogue to show character
- I see how writers use the past and present tenses in stories

LEVEL 5

- I can identify and comment on the effect of similes
- I understand how word choices affect tone and exact meaning
- I can comment on how writers vary sentence length for effect
- I understand the use of formality and informality in dialogue
- I can comment on the use of past and present tense in stories

Chapter 5

AF6 Identify and comment on writers' purposes and viewpoints, and the overall effect of the text on the reader

This chapter is going to show you how to

- Write and talk about the **purpose** of a text
- Write and talk about the **viewpoint** of the writer
- Use your understanding of **viewpoint** in your own writing
- Write and talk about the **effect** of a text on the reader
- Write and talk about the **effect** of a writer's word choices

What's it all about?

What does the writer want to achieve and how have they tried to do this?

This lesson will
- help you identify and understand the main purposes of a text.

Every text is written for a reason. When we talk about the **purpose** of a text we mean the reason why it was created.

A text might have several different **purposes**. For example, a magazine article might be written to entertain you *and* to inform you about an important issue.

Getting you thinking

Many texts are written to persuade us to buy things.

- With a partner, make a list of three different texts you have seen this week which were trying to persuade you to buy something. For instance:

1 Bus stop poster

Now you try it

Here is the home page of a website about the film, *The Boy in the Striped Pajamas*.

1 Write a list of the things that tell you this is a website. Try to use technical terms if you can (the glossary will help you).

2 Choose three of the features you have listed. What job do they do in this text? Explain your ideas to your partner or write them next to your list. For instance:

> *Links to other pages – help the reader to explore the website.*

3 Why do you think the filmmakers produced a website like this? Work with your partner to make a list of ideas.

4 Now point to two pieces of evidence in the text which show you that you're right.

Tell your partner why you have chosen these features.

5 Write your answer to this question: **Why was the website produced?**

You could start: *One purpose of this website is to...*

Support each point with evidence from the text. In your next sentence explain which piece of evidence you have chosen.

Start your sentence: *I know this because...*

Glossary

links: words or pictures which take you to another page

downloads: information and pictures which you can save on your computer

graphics: pictures

Development activity

Compare your paragraph with the Level 4 paragraph below.

> One purpose of this website is to persuade people to watch the film. I know this because there is a quotation from a newspaper saying the film is 'beautifully and sensitively directed.'

Point to where this student has:

- identified the **purpose** of the text
- given evidence for their ideas.

Now look at the paragraph you wrote. Do you need to make any changes to reach Level 4?

Remember

Every text is written for a reason, and as good readers we need to work out what that reason is!

Check your progress

LEVEL 3	I can make comments about the purpose of a text
LEVEL 4	I can identify the main purpose of a text
LEVEL 5	I can clearly identify the main purpose of a text and start to explain how I know this

2 Write and talk about the viewpoint of the writer

This lesson will
● help you to identify and understand the main viewpoints in a text.

A writer can shape how we feel about a character by looking at things from their **viewpoint**.

We need to spot the writer's **viewpoint** to understand how they are trying to make us feel.

Getting you thinking

Sometimes a writer uses a character's voice to tell the story and sometimes they tell the story with their own voice.

Look at the sentences below. Point to the sentence you think is:

● written from the writer's viewpoint
● written from a character's viewpoint.

> I watched the clouds pass above my head and longed to know what it would be like to fly through them.

> As he lay on the grass watching the clouds float past, he wondered what it would be like to fly through them.

How does it work?

'**I** watched the clouds pass above **my** head and longed to know what it would be like to fly through them.' ——— this tells us that the passage is written from a **first person viewpoint**

'As **he** lay on the grass watching the clouds float past, he wondered what it would be like to fly through them.' ——— this tells us that the passage is written from a **third person viewpoint**

Now you try it

Look back at the picture of the two boys on page 56.

Here is an extract from the novel that the film was based on. We are going to work out which of the boys' **viewpoints** we are looking from.

> When Bruno first approached the boy, he was sitting cross-legged on the ground, staring at the dust beneath him. However, after a moment he looked up and Bruno saw his face. It was quite a strange face too. His skin was almost the colour of grey, but not quite like any grey that Bruno had ever seen before. He had very large eyes and they were the colour of caramel sweets; the whites were very white, and when the boy looked at him all Bruno could see was an enormous pair of sad eyes looking back.
>
> John Boyne, *The Boy in the Striped Pyjamas*

- Is John Boyne telling the story as one of the characters or with his own voice?
- Which one of the boys in the picture is Bruno? Give three reasons for your decision.

Development activity

1 Write the author's name (John Boyne) on the top of a sticky note.

2 Stick the note on the picture of Bruno and Shmuel (the other boy) where you think that the writer would be standing, or sitting, as he wrote this. Draw an arrow to show which way he is looking.

Explain to your partner why you have made this choice.

3 Choose a short phrase from the text which shows you where the writer is looking from.

Write the words on the sticky note. Tell your partner why you chose this phrase.

4 Write a sentence explaining the writer's viewpoint. Use this structure:

John Boyne is writing from the point of view of...

Stick your note underneath your sentence to give evidence for your statement.

Remember

In fiction, writers use viewpoint to influence how we feel about characters or events.

3 Use your understanding of viewpoint in your own writing

This lesson will
- help you understand and use viewpoints.

On these pages you are going to think more about the writer's **viewpoint** and show your understanding in your own writing.

Getting you thinking

As a writer, you can use viewpoint to influence how the reader thinks and feels.

1 With your partner, look at the opening page of a story you have been reading in your English lessons.

Can you work out whether the story is
a written from the writer's viewpoint
b written from a character's viewpoint?

2 Now look back at the picture and the passage from *The Boy in the Striped Pyjamas* on pages 56 and 59.

Re-stick your sticky note where you thought the writer's **viewpoint** was and re-read the sentences you wrote about it to remind yourself of why you made this decision.

How does it work?

The writer is telling the story in the **third person** but it is written from Bruno's **viewpoint**.

Now you try it

Imagine you are telling the story from the **viewpoint** of Shmuel (the other boy).

Point to a place in the text where things would be written differently. Tell your partner how Shmuel would have seen it.

Use the picture to help you too.

Development activity APP

1 Write a short passage from Shmuel's viewpoint describing Bruno coming towards you and sitting down.

   Remember that John Boyne is telling the story with his own voice so you need to write **in the third person** using 'he', not with Shmuel's voice.

   You could begin:

   > Shmuel was sitting by the fence, one hot, dusty afternoon, when he saw someone coming towards him. It was...

2 Use another sticky note. Put your name on it and stick it to the picture where you imagined you were standing (or sitting) when you wrote the passage.

   Draw an arrow to show which way you were looking.

   Now choose a phrase from your writing which shows this. Write it on the sticky note.

Remember

As a writer you can influence what the reader thinks or feels.

3 Is your viewpoint different from John Boyne's? Write two sentences explaining your answer using this structure:

   > My viewpoint is from _____, whereas John Boyne's viewpoint is from _____. You can see this when...

'A small wonder of a book ... A particular historical moment, one that cannot be told too often'
GUARDIAN

60308

THE BOY IN THE STRIPED PYJAMAS
JOHN BOYNE

This lesson will

● help you make a personal response to a text.

These pages will help you to talk and write about the way a text can make the reader feel. We will be working with pictures and a written text.

Getting you thinking

Looking at a picture or reading a text can make us feel lots of emotions. We might find it funny, or it might make us feel sad or scared.

1 Make a list of some of the emotions a text or picture might make you feel.

2 Now use a thesaurus to find a few different ways of describing each emotion. For example,

Sad = miserable, upset, tearful.

3 Now look at these three pictures. Which of the lions do you like best?

4 Explain to your partner why you like this lion.

How does the picture make you feel? Use some of the words that you listed in the first activity in your answer and some of the phrases below.

I like this lion best because...

> *it makes me feel...*
> *I find it...*
> *the picture makes it look...*

Now you try it

Look again at the pictures. This time decide which lion is most frightening. Think of three reasons for your choice.

Now explain to your partner why this lion is scarier than the others.

Begin by saying: *This lion is the most frightening because...*

For the picture you have chosen, write down one thing that

- you like about the picture
- you don't like about the picture
- the picture reminds you of
- you would like to ask about the picture.

Development activity

Here is a verse from a **monologue** poem called 'The Lion and Albert'.

> There were one great big lion called Wallace
> His nose were all covered with scars
> He lay in a **somnolent** posture
> With the side of his face to the bars.

Glossary

monologue: a text written to be read aloud by one speaker

somnolent: sleepy or lazy

1 Which picture do you think best matches the description of Wallace the lion? Choose two or three words from the poem that tell you this.

2 Write a sentence answering each of these questions:
   a Which words has the writer chosen to make this lion seem frightening?
   b Which words has the writer chosen to make this lion seem lazy?
   c What does the lion's name make you feel about him?

Remember

Think about the choices the artist or writer has made.

Check your progress

LEVEL 3	I was able to say how I felt about the lion
LEVEL 4	I was able to say how the writer wanted me to feel about the lion
LEVEL 5	I was able to identify the way the writer chose words to create an effect on the reader

63

This lesson will
- show you how to support your personal response to a text with textual reference.

Writers choose their words carefully to achieve their purpose. This might be to make the reader think or feel something, or to create a picture in the reader's mind.

Getting you thinking

In this poem, Mr and Mrs Ramsbottom are on holiday in Blackpool with their son, Albert. They have decided to visit the zoo.

The Lion and Albert

There were one great big lion called Wallace
His nose were all covered with scars
He lay in a **somnolent** posture
With the side of his face to the bars.

Now Albert had heard about lions
How they were ferocious and wild
And to see Wallace lying so peaceful
Well... it didn't seem right to the child.

So straight 'way the brave little feller
Not showing a morsel of fear
Took his stick with the **horse's head handle**
And pushed it in Wallace's ear!

You could see that the lion didn't like it
For giving a kind of a roll
He pulled Albert inside the cage with 'im
And swallowed the little lad... whole!

Marriott Edgar

Glossary

somnolent: sleepy or lazy

horse's head handle: a handle shaped like a horse's head

Hear the poem read aloud.

- Is this a funny event or is it very sad?
- Which lines made you laugh? Find them in the text and talk to your partner about what makes them funny.

How does it work?

You might have chosen this line:

And pushed it in Wallace's ear!

What makes this funny?

a Is it the name of the lion? (Wallace doesn't sound very tough!)

b Is it the exclamation mark? (This shows that it was a surprising thing to do.)

c Is it the picture that it creates in your head? (Have you ever wanted to do something like that?)

Now you try it

Copy out this table. Find three words or phrases that the writer uses to describe Albert and the lion. For each one, explain how they make you feel about the character.

Albert		The lion	
Words or phrases	How they make you feel about him	Words or phrases	How they make you feel about him

Development activity

Who do you feel is most to blame for Albert being eaten?

You can use this structure if you like:

I think that the character who is to blame for Wallace eating Albert is...

I think this because...

Remember

Writers choose their **words** carefully, adopt a **viewpoint** and shape the way a text **sounds** to influence how the reader feels or thinks.

Check your progress

LEVEL 3 I am able to give a personal opinion about the text

LEVEL 4 I am able to make comments about the effect of the text on a reader

LEVEL 5 I am able to identify the effect on the reader and give some evidence for my ideas

Level Booster

LEVEL 3

- I can talk about the purpose of a text
- I can give my opinion about a character or place in a text

LEVEL 4

- I can identify the main purpose of a text
- I can comment on the writer's viewpoint
- I can comment on the way the writer makes the reader feel
- I can give some evidence for my ideas

LEVEL 5

- I can identify what the writer is trying to achieve (the writer's purpose)
- I can identify the writer's viewpoint
- I can identify the effect a text has on the reader
- I can explain my ideas

Chapter 6

AF7 Relate texts to their social, cultural and historical traditions

This chapter is going to show you how to

- Identify different time, place and social settings in texts
- Identify character and setting in texts
- Compare texts in the same genre
- Identify character and setting in texts from different times

What's it all about?

Texts vary with time, place and genre. It is important to be aware of these contexts in your reading.

This lesson will

● show you how to spot the times and places of different texts

Books are set in different **times**, **places and societies**. These settings can be real or imaginary. If you can **comment** simply on the effect of different **time**, **place or social settings**, you are reading at Level 4.

Getting you thinking

Read this description of warrior training:

> I held my arm towards him and he placed the dry leaf upon my skin. So intent was I, so **determined** that I must succeed in this trial, that my arm seemed to grow large and heavy. The nerves prickled at the leaf's rough dryness. Next I felt the burning heat of the flaming stick he **bore** towards me. He lit the leaf and my body **surged** in response, wanting to **quench** the flame that licked and curled around the leaf. The pain rose and rose and threatened to **engulf** me. The only way to **endure** was to pass beyond it, to a different way of being.
>
> *Apache: Girl Warrior* by Tanya Landman

Glossary

determined: sure

bore: brought

surged: moved forward like a wave

quench: crush, put out

engulf: swamp, overcome

endure: survive

In threes, imagine this training is taking place in a modern school.

● One of you is the older Apache; one is the trainee. Mime the 'lesson'. (Apaches never make unnecessary sound so this should be in silence.)

● A modern school inspector enters at the end of the mime. At this point, sound returns. The inspector asks what on earth is going on.

● Come out of role. What do you think of the Apache training? Could it ever happen in your school?

Now you try it

In the novel *King of Shadows* a boy called Nat Field has gone to bed with a fever in 1999. He wakes up in Shakespeare's England!

> I woke up with my face in the pillow, and even before I opened my eyes I knew something was wrong. My face and my body told me that I was lying on a different pillow, and a different bed; hard, both of them, and crackly. The bed was really uncomfortable. I moved my hip; surely it wasn't even a bed, but a mattress on the floor.
>
> 'How do you?' he said. 'Is your fever less?'
>
> I stared at him. 'Who are you?' I said
>
> 'Harry of course. Have your wits gone, Nat. You look strange. Dear Lord, I was afraid you had the plague.'
>
> I lay very still with my senses telling me that I had gone mad. The plague? Nobody's had the plague for centuries.

● What makes Nat think he has woken up in the past? Try to find at least three things.

Development activity

Using your list, write three sentences explaining how we know Nat is in Shakespearean England. Start:

> Nat wakes up in Shakespeare's time. We can tell this because...
> Another thing that tells us this is...

Check your progress

LEVEL 3 I can sometimes spot time and place in texts

LEVEL 4 I can spot previous times and places in texts

LEVEL 5 I can identify how a text relates to its time and place

This lesson will
- show you how to spot character and setting in a detective story

Texts are made up of different **strands**. People in a story are called **characters**. Where a story happens is called the **setting**. We also need to think about how the writer **presents** the characters and setting.

If you can comment on such features, you are reading at Level 4.

Getting you thinking

Look at this opening of an Agatha Christie detective novel.

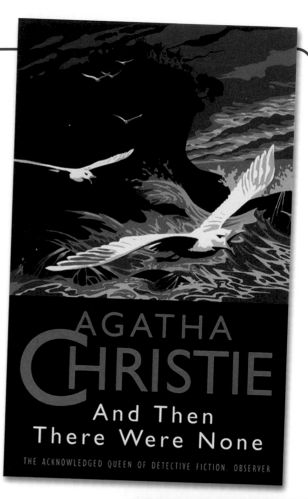

> In the corner of a first class smoking carriage, Mr Justice Wargrave, lately retired **from the bench**, puffed at a cigar and ran an interested eye through the political news of the Times. He laid the paper down and glanced out of the window (of the train). They were running now through Somerset. He glanced at his watch – another two hours to go.

- Do you think it is set nearer (a) 2007 (b) 1937 (c) 1797 or (d) 1067?
- Where do you think this story is set?
- What do we learn about the character?
- Which word do you think sums up the mood of this first paragraph?

Funny   Cosy   Scary   Tense   Old-fashioned

Glossary

from the bench: from being a Judge

Now you try it

Here is the opening of another Agatha Christie novel.
Hear it read aloud and then discuss the questions below.

> Mrs Ferrars died on the night of the 16th–17th
> September – a Thursday. I was sent for at eight
> o'clock on the morning of Friday 17th. There was
> nothing to be done. She had been dead some hours.
>
> *The Murder of Roger Ackroyd*

1 Two **characters** are introduced here. Who are they?

2 What, if anything, are we told about each **character**?

3 What do you think the person who is telling the story does for a living?

4 Are we told anything about the **time or place setting**?

5 How are the events **presented**? Would you say the way the story is told is: Emotional? Angry? Practical? Medical? Matter of Fact? Cold? Amused? Personal?

Development activity

Here is part of the second paragraph of *The Murder of Roger Ackroyd*. Hear it read aloud.

> It was just a few minutes after nine when I reached
> home once more. I opened the front door with my
> latchkey. To tell the truth, I was considerably upset and
> worried. I am not going to pretend that at that moment
> I **foresaw** the events of the next few weeks. But my
> **instinct** told me there were **stirring** times ahead.

Glossary

foresaw: knew in advance
what would happen

instinct: gut feeling

stirring: exciting

In pairs, focus on either **character** or **setting**. Find as
much information as you can from the text.

Then write two sentences beginning:

> *We learn that the character is... We also learn
> that the character...*
> *The place setting is ... The time setting is ...*

Check your progress

LEVEL 3	I can read for simple character and setting
LEVEL 4	I can read for character and (time and place) setting
LEVEL 5	I can explain conventions of character and setting in texts

3 Compare texts in the same genre

This lesson will

● show you how to identify and compare pirate stories

This means you need to **compare characters**, **setting**, and how they are **presented** across stories of **the same genre** or type. In these pages we will be looking at different pirate stories.

Getting you thinking

● Do you know who these two characters are?

● What do you know about them?

● What would you expect to happen in a pirate story or film?

Now read the following paragraph. How do we know this is a pirate story?

You never forget the first attack. I was **cotton-mouthed** and terrified, standing at the ready, waiting to hear the two ships grind and splinter together. The waiting is the worst of it. I've seen strong men turn pale as porridge, and dash to the heads to relieve themselves, or vomit over the side. No-one makes any comment. No-one mocks or jeers at them, even these men who seem to laugh in the face of death itself. They stare straight ahead, gripping weapons. Sometimes, Broom [the captain] ordered drums and cymbals to add to the **clamour**, or the cannons fired, filling the air with the reek of powder, so we boarded **the prize** through blinding **billows** of smoke. Once on the ship, then it was different. We would board with reckless boldness, and if the prize **offered resistance**, it was kill or be killed.

Celia Rees, *Pirates*

Now you try it

Read aloud this passage from a play version of *Treasure Island* by Robert Louis Stevenson.

Jemmy Rathbone is being chased by pirates around the deck of a ship.

HANDS	Grab 'im
DEATH	'old 'im!
HANDS	Trap 'im between you, ya dogs.
MERRY	You miserable dolts! How far can he get? We're on a Ship!
BONNY	I got him!
BLACK DOG	Got him!
RATHBONE	*(caught)* Ahhhhhhhhhhhhhhh!

*The **pirates** tackle him and pin his arms behind him.*

BLACK DOG   Bonny, hold him down!

> **Glossary**
>
> **fo'c's'le:** forecastle, the front part of the ship where the crew live
>
> **parries:** blocks

***Captain James Flint** steps out of the **fo'c's'le**. He looks evil beyond description. He has a hideous scar on one side of his face. He has a mop of greasy red hair sticking out of the sides of his black, tattered hat. He's missing three fingers from his left hand.*

RATHBONE   Oh, Cap'n Flint! Thank God above you's 'ere. They was gonna kill me, Cap'n. Kill me fer nothing!

***Israel Hands** brings his cutlass down towards **Rathbone**'s head and **Captain Flint** **parries** the blow with a flick of his wrist, saving **Rathbone**'s life.*

- Note down any pirate words and phrases you spot.
- With a partner, make a comment for each phrase you chose. What makes it a pirate phrase?

Development activity (APP)

Here are three pirate objects:

a locked treasure chest   an eye patch   a crumpled map.

1 Imagine the map shows the place where treasure is hidden. In pairs, tell each other a story about the pirates and why they hid the treasure. Who did the eye patch belong to?

> **Remember**
>
> Your pirate setting and pirate words and phrases!

Check your progress

LEVEL 3	I can spot some pirate story features
LEVEL 4	I can compare pirate features in two pirate stories
LEVEL 5	I can explain something about the conventions of pirate stories

This lesson will
- show you how to trace how war texts reflect different war periods

The **strands** we have been exploring – **characters** and **setting** – can be found in the earliest texts ever written. They can also be found today. A Level 4 reader needs to be able to recognise how these same strands **vary in texts from different times**.

Getting you thinking

Here helicopter pilot Ed Macy describes his experiences of fighting the Taliban in Afghanistan.

'PUTS YOU RIGHT IN THE COCKPIT . . . AWESOME.'
ANDY MCNAB

ED MACY

APACHE

THE BLAZING TRUE BESTSELLER FROM THE HEART OF AFGHANISTAN

'Ugly Five Zero, Knight Rider. **Intelligence** from higher; there are enemy in a compound by the canal two hundred metres north of the original target.'

'Ugly Five Zero. Running in from the west with Hellfire. Ugly Five One you take that target; I've got two buildings to finish off here.'

There was an awful lot of smoke and dust in the air so Carl swung us away and over to the west side of the canal. It gave me a better view.

The new compound was the furthest north of a cluster of three. We held off 2,500 metres south-west of it, so as not to spook the enemy.

I picked up a series of white shapes on my **FLIR** and zoomed in: four men stood in a group against the high compound wall. One had what appeared to be an **RPG** alongside him. Two others had a moped in front of them. A donkey flicked its tail **disconsolately** in the top left-hand corner of the compound, thirty metres to their west. I needed to confirm that this was the correct target.

- What details in the passage tell you that this is a modern-day battle?

Glossary

FLIR: an infra-red device used to give the viewer a thermal picture and to provide night vision at long distances

intelligence: information from an aircraft above them

RPG: a rocket-propelled grenade: a handheld, shoulder-launched weapon used against tanks, vehicles and buildings

disconsolately: sadly

Now you try it

This poem, written in 1854, describes the Battle of Balaclava in the Crimean War.

Cannon to right of them,
Cannon to left of them,
Cannon behind them
Volley'd and thunder'd;
Storm'd at with **shot** and **shell**,
While horse and hero fell,
They that had fought so well
Came thro' the jaws of Death,
Back from the mouth of Hell,
All that was left of them,
Left of six hundred.

Alfred Lord Tennyson,
'The Charge of the Light Brigade'

Glossary

shot: fired at close range, grapeshot turned cannons into giant machine guns.

shell: bomb-canisters fired at medium range.

- What clues can you find in the text to tell you that this is not a modern war?
- What is different from the description of a modern war? What is the same?

Development activity

In groups, imagine you are transported back in time to Balaclava. Use the picture and the poem to guide you.

Make a tableau of yourselves as soldiers in that war setting. Try to select features – like cannon or horses – that are very different from today's wars.

Once you've made your tableau, get your teacher to take a photo.

Then devise a caption that sums up the writer's attitude to the characters and setting: for instance, *Sent to their deaths*.

Check your progress

LEVEL 3 I can spot some historical features in a war text

LEVEL 4 I can identify context (a different time) in a war text

LEVEL 5 I can explain the context (different time, different war) in war texts

Level Booster

LEVEL 3

- I can make simple connections between texts
- I can identify similarities in character types between texts
- I can recognise some time and place settings
- I can identify similarities in plot and topic between texts

LEVEL 4

- I can identify different time, place and social settings in texts
- I can identify character and setting in texts from different times and places
- I can compare texts in the same genre
- I can compare settings in texts from different times

LEVEL 5

- I can identify narrative (and other) conventions in texts
- I can identify texts in context (time, place and social setting)
- I can compare and contrast narrative (and other) conventions in texts
- I can make some explanation of how context (time, place and social setting) affects the way we read
- I can make some explanation of how context affects the way texts are written

Chapter 7

Longer texts and reading activities

What's it all about?

Bringing all the Assessment Focuses together.

Look at these three pages from a website

 Adventure, freedom, friends!
unmissable adventure holidays for 7-17 year olds

Home   Schools   Groups   **Adventure Holidays**   Families   Working with PGL   About us   Contact us   My PGL

Holidays | Centres | 7-17s | Parents | DVDs | Activities

Home :

Multi Activity

This is our most popular holiday! Multi Activity challenges you to pack as much as you can into your holiday.

| **Whats it all about?** | More info | Activities | Comments | Examples |

Print Friendly View

Six days of multi activity

Test your skills across lots of different activities so you'll never be bored! Whether you are staying for a week or a mini break you'll have a great time.

Can you believe that there are over 50 different activities to try?

Activities on land, on the water, some you have always wanted to try and some you have never heard of before! You will get to try loads of different activities from motorbiking to fencing and abseiling to mountain biking.

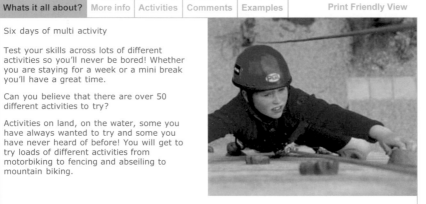

 Adventure, freedom, friends!
unmissable adventure holidays for 7-17 year olds

Home   Schools   Groups   **Adventure Holidays**   Families   Working with PGL   About us   Contact us   My PGL

Holidays | Centres | 7-17s | Parents | DVDs | Activities

Home :

Multi Activity

This is our most popular holiday! Multi Activity challenges you to pack as much as you can into your holiday.

| Whats it all about? | **More info** | Activities | Comments | Examples |

Print Friendly View

A Multi Activity holiday is the ideal choice if you have never been to a PGL centre before. You can discover what you enjoy most, what you are good at and challenge yourself, all day, every day. There are so many activities, we know that it's impossible to fit them all into one holiday – but you won't mind because you will be raring to come back and try the rest! In fact, in the meantime, we will have probably added some more to the list!

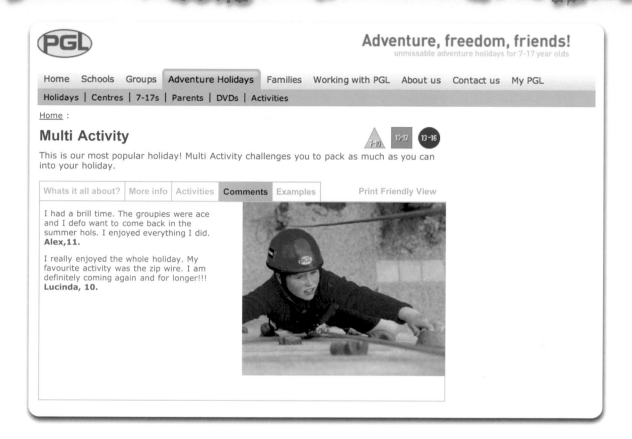

AF 2 How many different activities are there on the adventure holidays? What four activies are listed?

AF 3 What can you discover about the type of people who might find PGL activity centres appealing? Make sure you refer to the text in your answer.

AF 4 How does the PGL website use its layout and structure to make the material easy for readers to follow?

AF 5 What kind of language is used on the website? Is it

  a chatty   d difficult to understand
  b friendly   e simple
  c formal   f unfriendly

Is the language on any of the screens different from the others?

AF 6 What is the purpose of this website? Try to give examples from the text to back up your ideas and explain why you chose them.

AF 7 How can you tell this is a modern-day text?

The little smasher

While Andy Murray was baring his biceps, another Brit was quietly winning Wimbledon. Last month, the junior champion won her first pro tournament – and she's still only 14

Britain's Laura Robson kisses her trophy after winning the Wimbledon girl's singles final.

Early in the summer, sports agent Abigail Tordoff was talking to *The Observer* about one of her clients. 'Definitely one to look out for in the future,' she said. 'In a couple of years she will really be big.' Then her 14-year-old protégée won Wimbledon. Laura Robson wasn't one for the future any more.

It was the first time in 24 years, since Annabel Croft, that a home player had won the Girls' Singles. Even more impressive, Robson – who lives just down the road from the All England Club – was the youngest player in the competition.

With her attractive shot-making, and equally appealing personality, Robson, currently the British No. 15, has given the women's game a bright hope. This autumn, she took her first steps on the professional tour. Within six weeks she won her first tournament, an ITF event in Sunderland. Her first winner's cheque came to £772.

'2008 has been a great year for me,' she says now. 'Winning Wimbledon was such an amazing experience, especially because I didn't expect to win it. It was weird to see myself on TV and in the paper!' Still, Robson seems to have handled it all with an endearingly cheeky spirit.

Emma John, *The Observer*, Sunday 23 November 2008

AF 2 Find three pieces of information about Laura Robson.

AF 3 How does the writer suggest that Laura is a success? You should write about

- the headline
- the photograph and caption
- the words the writer uses to describe Laura
- the statistics that are used.

Make sure that you refer to the text in your answer.

AF 4 What tells you that this is a newspaper article and not some other kind of text?

AF 5 Why is so much of the article in speech marks?

Why does the writer include other people's opinions of Laura?

AF 6 Look at the first three paragraphs of the article. How does the writer want us to feel about Laura Robson? Try to explain why you think this. What words and phrases tell you this?

AF 7 How does the writer draw attention to Laura Robson's age and the fact she is a girl in the way she presents her success? You should think about

- the time
- the place (Britain)
- the social setting (the 'women's game').

How do phrases like 'the little smasher' and 'attractive' reflect Laura's age and/or the fact she is a girl?

Scene One

The Prince and his servant are lost in the dark woods.

Prince Kano (*worried*)	We've spent the whole day trying to find our way out of the wood.
Servant (*surprised*)	I'm sorry, your highness, I really thought I knew these woods. (*pause*) They seem to have changed.
Prince Kano (*annoyed*)	How can they change? Do the trees move or something?
Servant	There are strange tales about these woods, your highness.
Prince Kano	Strange tales? What are we, babies? I don't believe in strange tales.
Servant (*looking up*)	I think it's getting dark. Shouldn't we find somewhere to sleep?
Prince Kano (*still annoyed*)	No, you blockhead. The wolves will eat us alive. We need to keep on the move. We need to find our way out of here.

Scene Two

The Prince and his servant notice a small clearing. A man is cooking food on an open fire.

Servant (*pointing*)	Look, there is a man cooking food. He's covered in a hooded cloak, so we can't see his face. I'm scared!
Prince Kano	He'll know the way out of here, he's a woodsman. (*relieved*) At last! (*The Prince runs over to the man wearing the hooded cloak.*) Good friend, I'll give you what you will ask. (*jiggles his pockets*) Guide me to where I live.

The man pulls back his hood. There is an empty space where his face should have been.

Servant (*runs off*)	I'm going – better to be a live coward than a dead hero!

The Prince runs in the opposite direction.

Scene Three

The Prince wanders through the wood all night. Finally, he sees a large clearing. There are houses, people. They all wear hoods.

Prince (*to himself*)	I'm frightened. Why do these people all wear hoods?

The Prince notices a church.

                    Ah, a church always offers comfort.

The Prince runs to the church and opens the door. Inside, monks are praying.

Prince *(to himself)*   I'll speak to one of these monks. He'll know how I can get home.

The Prince taps a monk on the shoulder.

                    I've seen a dreadful thing. I'm afraid – scared stiff.

Monk *(looking down)*   What did you see, my son?

Prince Kano   I saw a man who's face was like …

The monk draws back his hood. He seems to hiss and point to where his face should have been.

Monk   Like this?

The Prince faints.

Adapted from the poem 'Prince Kano' by Edward Lowbury.

AF 2   What do we find out about the four characters in this play? Write a sentence about each one.

AF 3   In this play, the Prince is going through a challenging experience. Can you work out how he is feeling each time he speaks? For each thing he says, draw a thought bubble and write down what you think he is feeling or thinking.

AF 4   There are three scenes in this play. Think about what happens in each scene and decide why you think each new scene is started.

AF 5   Look at the words written in italics. What do you think these words are? Why do you think the writer includes them?

AF 6   The play is written from Prince Kano's viewpoint. How do you feel about the Prince? Do you like or dislike him?

              Find examples from the play to explain your ideas.

AF 7   How do we know the play is set in a strange world? Think about
- the characters
- the setting
- what the characters say.

              Where do you think the Prince is? Has he wandered into an alternative world?

Dark Woods is certainly a strange place to visit. If you meet the people from Dark Woods City you will notice that they don't have faces. However, they are shy but friendly.

If you're **invited into their homes**, remove your shoes at the door and cover your face by wearing a hoodie and a scarf. These people are afraid of faces and they hate noise. If you need to look at them, **don't look directly at them**. They have eyes on their necks and they never stare!

Dark Woods people sing but their sad songs sound like hissing snakes. They enjoy singing and will sing for hours at a time. It's a pity they can't sing in tune!

When **eating**, Dark Woods people grab food in their right hands and stuff the food into the top of their long tunics. If you are lucky, you might see their long necks reach out to grab the food. They like to slurp and belch as the food slithers down their throats. You must try and do the same, or you might offend them. **Pretend you don't have a face**, or you might make them afraid.

AF 2 Describe a person from Dark Woods City.

AF 3 What do you think of Dark Woods people? Explain why you think as you do.

AF 4 Look at the four paragraphs. What is each paragraph about? Why have some words been highlighted in the text?

AF 5 Which words do you find interesting in this travel guide? How do they bring the description of Dark Woods and its people to life? Pick out any words you do not know and look them up in a dictionary.

AF 6 Why do you think the writer wrote this travel guide? Does it make you want to visit Dark Woods or was the guide written for another reason?

AF 7 What does this guide tell us about Dark Woods?

You should write about

- the key differences between Dark Woods and where you live.
- whether this guide is fact or fiction? How do you know?

Oh, where was that stupid boy? Mel peered into the trees on each side of the winding path.

Coldharbour Woods were huge, stretching on for miles around, but people only walked on the outskirts. A few wide paths had been cleared and given names, like The Sika Trail and The Silver Birch Walk. Some narrower tracks had been carved out over the years as people took shortcuts. Tom had gone off on one of these, and he seemed to have vanished into thin air.

'Tom!' Mel called yet again.

She listened for a reply, but none came. The only sounds were the rustling of dead leaves on the ground, and now and then the harsh cawing of rooks. Mel shivered again and glanced nervously behind her. She couldn't shake off the feeling that someone was watching her, and it made her heart thump in her chest. She had to admit that she was beginning to get frightened, out here in the woods on her own. Why weren't there a few more people around? There'd been loads of families when they started their walk.

Mel jumped as a twig cracked loudly nearby. A cold hand of fear clutched at her stomach. She whirled around, her eyes darting from tree to tree, trying to see something – anything – only to be met by a thick wall of branches.

And then she saw him.

Tom was propped up against a tree trunk at the side of the track. His head was on one side, blond hair flopping over his face. Strange, half-strangled noises were coming out of his mouth.

And a hand was around his neck, the fingers pressing hard against his throat.

AF 2 Who is Mel looking for? Find two sentences that tell us who she is looking for.

AF 3 Write down how you think Mel feels about being alone in the woods. Which words and phrases suggest this to you?

AF 4 Re-read the story. What is happening in each paragraph? Why do you think paragraphs five and seven are so short?

AF 5 The writer uses words and phrases carefully to help us imagine what it is like to be alone in the woods.

Read the sentence below:

'There were dead leaves on the ground and you could hear rooks.'

This does not sound very exciting. Look at the revised sentence. How does the writer make it more exciting than the first sentence?

'The only sounds were the rustling of dead leaves on the ground, and now and then the harsh cawing of rooks.'

AF 6 How does the writer make you feel at the end of this extract? Explain your answer by referring to the text.

AF 7 What kind of place is Coldharbour Woods? What makes it feel scary?

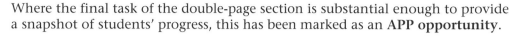
Teacher Guide

Where the final task of the double-page section is substantial enough to provide a snapshot of students' progress, this has been marked as an **APP opportunity**.

Each double-page section ends with a **Check your progress** box. This offers a levelled checklist against which students can self- or peer-assess their final piece of writing from the **Development** or, occasionally, **Now you try it** section.

The end of chapter **Level Booster** is a less task-specific checklist of the skills students need to master to reach Level 3, 4 and 5. It can be used to help students see the level they are working at currently and to visualise what they need to do to make progress.

To the Teacher

The general aim of these books is the practical and everyday application of **Assessment for Learning (AfL)**: to ensure every child knows how they are doing and what they need to do to improve. The specific aim is to support **APP (Assessing Pupils' Progress)**: the 'periodic' view of progress by teacher and learner.

The books empower the student by modelling the essential skills needed at each level, and by allowing them to practise and then demonstrate independently what they know and can do across every reading and writing (APP) strand. They support the teacher by providing opportunities to gather and review secure evidence of progress in each **Assessment Focus (AF)**. Where appropriate (and especially at lower levels) the books facilitate teacher **scaffolding** of such learning and assessment.

The series offers exercises that we hope will not only help students add descriptive power and nuance to their vocabulary but also expand the grammatical constructions they can access and use: above all, the ability to write and read in sentences (paragraphs, texts) – to think consciously in complete thoughts.

We hope we can enrich how students read, recognising not just the texts they are decoding but also the contexts in which they read them. Our extracts cannot replace longer texts. The longer reading passages in our Reading books, with questions that cover all the AFs working together, are a crucial acknowledgement of this. Each AF is a provisional isolation of various emphases, to be practised and mastered before bringing it back to the real reading and writing of whole texts in which all these – suitably polished – skills can be applied.

Gareth Calway
Series Editor

1 Find and comment on relevant points in a text

As a quick-fire starter, ask students how they would read the TV listings to find out when their favourite programme was on. Would they read the page line by line, from top to bottom, as they would a novel? Explain that we read different types of text in different ways depending on what we are trying to find out.

Getting you thinking

Explain to students that when they are answering a reading question like this, it can be helpful to skim over the text first. Then, once they are clear what the text is about, they should look at the question and read through the text more carefully to work out the answer.

Development

As a possible extension, ask students to complete this task for homework:

Find out the key points: When looking for key points in a text, practice makes perfect. Find three types of text from the world around you. These can be leaflets, newspapers, notices, school letters or even a cornflake box. Use your skills to work out what the three most important or key points are for that text.

1 Look at the way each text is laid out. Does the font size, use of bold or colour, or the layout give you any clue about which are the most important points?

2 Why has the writer or designer of this text used font size, bold, positioning or headlines to draw attention to these points?

2 Select relevant points from a range of sources

Getting you thinking

Allow plenty of time for reading through these texts. If necessary, read them aloud first with students to ensure understanding, explaining any unfamiliar words.

Now you try it

Allow plenty of time for this reading task and help students by reading the two reviews with them first.

As you feed back students' ideas, draw their attention to the two reviewers' agreement that the plot is thin and that the locations are great, and their disagreement over the villains and the car chases.

Extension

Students will need access to the internet for activity 2.

3 Support your ideas with detail, providing evidence to back up your points

Development Activities

● **Design.** *Your school has decided to update its image with a short leaflet to persuade parents to send their child to the school. In groups of four, draw a mock-up for what the leaflet should look like. Ensure you include a range of different design features, such as pictures and headings.*

For more challenge, ask students to write some of the text for this leaflet, as well as the headings for different sections and design features.

4 Find quotations to support your ideas

Extension

Here are two extension activities to help students understand how writers use language persuasively in charity advertisements and letters.

1 This activity will help students to explore how writers use adjectives, adverbs and verbs to influence how the reader feels.

Look again at the RSPCA leaflet. Find and write down words that describe the animals. These might be:

- **adjectives**, words that describe nouns (people, places, things). For example, 'a very **affectionate** puppy'.
- **nouns**, words that name people, places or things. These can be powerfully descriptive. For example, '**victims**'.

Now find and write down the words that describe the owners and what they did. These might be:

- **verbs**, doing words. For example, '**throw... away**'.
- **adverbs**, words that describe verbs. For example, '**callously** abandoned'.

- Finally, find a **verb** that describes what the RSPCA does.

Look at the words you've written down. How do these words make you feel about a) the animals, b) the people who mistreat animals, c) the RSPCA?

2 **Investigate.** Ask student to collect at least four other charity advertisements and bring them into class. In groups they should discuss each one and decide which they find most effective, using a chart like the one below:

Name of charity	
First line of the brochure	
Explain why this has been used	
Find a sentence that makes the reader feel sympathy	
What does this sentence mean?	

Chapter 2 AF3: deduce, infer or interpret information, events or ideas from texts

1 Make inferences from what you read

Getting you thinking

Model what 'reading between the lines' means for students with the example, sharing their ideas and inferences.

Now you try it

Read the text together as a class and then ask students to discuss the question in pairs.

If appropriate, share with students the two possible responses below and ask them what makes the second one better.

Here is one student's response:

I learn that a lady called Julie fell in love with a man called Allan.

This is true, but the student isn't inferring, simply repeating the facts.

You could answer the question more effectively by saying:

The opening to the article tells me that in life some people try really hard to find love. It also tells me that life can be very surprising and love can happen when you least expect it.

2 Make sense of information from different points in the text

Getting you thinking

- *What do you think the article is going to be about, based on the headline?*

This might be a good opportunity to explore the function of newspaper headlines with students. What kind of information do they usually give us? For instance, headlines often tell the reader what the story's about or intrigue the reader with a funny or puzzling title that makes them want to read on.

Now you try it

Read the article with students and ask them to think about what new information we learn here.

Development

2 *Finally, in small groups, look at this set of facts. It was included with the story about Zac's arrival at the premiere.*

Draw out with students that this is a different way of presenting information, using succinct bullet points rather than flowing prose. It gives us the vital stats about the film's success and is quite a common device in tabloid newspaper articles where space is at a premium.

3 Interpret what you read to make deductions about themes, characters and events (Part 1)

Explain to students that a book's blurb is a very short summary or taster of what happens in the story. It is usually printed on the back cover.

Getting you thinking

Explain to students that a **theme** is an idea or a topic area that often 'weaves' itself through a story. For example, a theme in *Romeo and Juliet* is 'young love'. A theme of *Batman* is 'the battle between good and evil'. Other themes could be things like 'mystery', 'childhood' or 'growing-up'.

Now you try it

Read the opening paragraph aloud and ask students to consider what its mood is.

Explain that the mood of a piece of writing can help us with the **theme** – if the mood is light-hearted and jokey then it is unlikely the novel will be about deep and serious matters.

Development

When you have thought about your answer, look at the two example answers below and then explain which one you think is best and why.

Draw out with students that the second answer is better because it

- pays close attention to what actually happens in the text
- makes links with the blurb
- poses questions which show the reader's engagement with the text.

In contrast, the first answer makes assumptions from the student's own experience, which are not rooted in the text.

4 Interpret what you read to make deductions about themes, characters and events (Part 2)

How does it work?

This list would be useful for students to refer to any time they need to think about character:

1 How the character behaves and what he or she does
2 What he or she says (about him / herself)
3 Any direct descriptions of the character by the writer.

Development

Explain to students the main events of the story so far, using the synopsis provided.

Every year Denny and his family are woken in the middle of Hallowe'en night by a mystery call, which his father usually answers. This year, Denny is determined to find out who is making the calls to his family's house and what his father's involvement was in the terrible fire that killed twenty-two children at The Globe theatre years ago. In the next extract, we see Denny is nervous about seeing the anniversary of the tragedy reported in the newspaper.

Then read aloud the extract(s) with students and ask them to answer the questions below.

Extension

In this unit, students have seen how the *themes* of the story (secrets, mystery, guilt, the past) are linked to *character* (Denny wanting to find out what happened but worried about what he will discover; Denny's dad blaming himself for something) and events (the secrets being revealed).

As an extension, ask students to think of any story they know well – it can be from a film, play, television series or book – and complete the task below.

Write one or two paragraphs in which you explain:

- *Who* the main character is
- *What* the main theme is (or themes)
- *What* the key events are.

If you can, try to say *how they are linked*.

You will need to use some of the connective words or phrases you have learned already. For example:

because, as a result of, consequently, so, also, in addition, moreover, later, afterwards, before, next .

5 Use skimming and scanning skills to locate information in a text

How does it work?

Ask students to suggest other occasions when they might use a) skimming and b) scanning.

Explain to students that when you skim and scan, you look for different sorts of information. You might use skimming when reading a newspaper to get an overall idea of the story. Scanning might be used when looking for someone's number in a telephone book.

Chapter 3 AF4 Identify and comment on the structure and organisation of texts

1 Identify whether a text is put together in a structured and organised way

Getting you thinking

Ask students to read the text aloud to each other in pairs and then discuss the question.

How does it work?

The student has focused on the build up to his trip and the trip itself, so the details he's included are mostly relevant. We probably don't need to know that he got up and had breakfast though!

Explain that the crucial problem is the order of the sentences and events.

Now you try it

Look back at what your friend wrote. Number each sentence in what you think should be the correct order.

It may help to provide photocopies of the extract for students to annotate.

When students have finished, ask them to swap their work with a partner and compare the decisions they made.

2 Recognise and understand the organisation of different texts

How does it work?

Emphasise to students that there are many **types of texts** and they come in different **modes**. Explain that a mode is the way information is communicated. This can be written, spoken or both (for example, a website might have video footage on it).

A text's organisational features reflect who is going to read the text and how they will read it.

Development

Explain that all texts have particular organisational features but many share the same ones. For example, a holiday brochure and a magazine about celebrities both have glossy photographs and are made up of lots of different 'bits' of writing.

3 Understand the use of headings and bullet points

How does it work?

Labels for the tags are as follows:

1 Name of the attraction written in an eye-catching way

2 Colourful image of kids having fun

3 Some information about Laser Zone and what it is.

4 A box with clear and easy-to-understand bullet points about how Laser Zone operates

5 Prices and opening times

6 Web address for Laser Zone.

Emphasise that bullet points are used for clarity and to make information easy to read.

The leaflet is eye-catching. It is colourful and energetic. The headings are used to

● tell us the name of the business

● tell us what the business does

● introduce the bullet points

The bullet points give customers an easy-to-read list of what makes *Laser Zone* fun and well organised.

Now you try it

In commenting on the headings, colours and fonts, encourage students to think about who the leaflet might be aimed at.

4 Understand the structure of stories

Getting you thinking

Most stories are organised in the following way:

Of course, not *all* stories work like this – and sometimes the exciting climax is the end of the story. Sometimes the character has to keep on facing problems (think of James Bond!).

Read the story together as a class. Then ask students to work in pairs to read the opening paragraphs again and answer the questions.

How does it work?

Ask students to read the beginning of this commentary about the introduction to the Tale:

> *I think the start of the Pardoner's Tale is when we are introduced to the three young men, what they are like and why they set out on their journey. I think the development of the story comes when they meet the old man…*

Then ask students: do you agree with this? Or do you think the problem – the real development comes later?

Extension

We have seen that the organisation of stories is not straightforward. Some of the class might have thought that the 'problem' was meeting the old man – others that it was 'how to deal with sharing out the gold'. There are no right answers here.

You may want to point out that some writers start with the problem. For example:

> *I stood in the empty house, and called again and again. But there was no answer. My brother had disappeared.*

Emphasise that not all stories will fit this model, but it is important to be aware of how a story's narrative is structured.

5 Comment on the form of a poem

Getting you thinking

Read the poem aloud or ask students to read it aloud to draw attention to the rhythm and rhyme.

Now you try it

Read the second poem aloud to students.

The key idea here is to make students see the relationship between a poem's form or shape and its meaning.

Try to get students to see how the form of the poem contributes to its mood or meaning. For instance, draw attention to

● **the repeated words in verses one and two** ('locked all locks', 'bolted bolts', 'hooked all hooks', 'checked and rechecked'). What do these repetitions suggest about the woman and how she feels about living alone?

- **the pause in the last line of verse two**. What is the effect of this pause and the doubting 'But'?

- **the question at the start of verse three**. How might this add to the creepy, paranoid mood of the poem?

- **the rhyming words in each verse**. How might these add to the feeling of being locked in?

Development

Make it clear that for Level 4 students only need to make some comments – they don't have to cover everything they discussed!

Chapter 4 AF5 Explain and comment on writers' use of language, including grammatical and literary features at word and sentence level

1 Comment on similes

Getting you thinking

Read the paragraph aloud to students. Read it again, this time asking students to look out for where the author has used the word 'like'.

Now you try it

Read the paragraph together. This time ask students to look out for the word 'as'.

You might like to point out that some similes play with words. Children's voices and church angels are 'high' in different ways!

2 Understand writers' word choices

In any text the writer has to decide what words to use. Your job is to understand why the writer has chosen these words – how they affect the meaning.

How does it work?

The writer's words show the difficulty and danger Peer and Hilde face.

Take the phrase 'bearing down'. This makes it sound like all the tons of rock overhead are pushing down on Peer, as if the mountain wants to crush him.

What about '*snatched* at the rocks'? Snatching is not relaxed. Would you say, 'I lay back by the pool and snatched another drink'?

Getting you thinking

Read the passage aloud with students.

Ask them to pay particular attention to what **verbs** the writer has chosen. Remind students that verbs are doing words denoting actions or states of being. For example, point out in the first sentence: 'Peer pushed', 'he snatched'.

How does it work?

Feed back students' ideas and model the examples given, 'snatched' and 'drummed'.

Now you try it

Encourage students to explain their preferences. Is the chosen word or phrase more precise?

Development

Explain that a writer's choice of nouns (words for things, people or places) and adjectives (words to describe nouns) also affects a text's meaning.

As an extension ask students to write a short paragraph explaining their group's decision. They should give at least one reason for this decision and find an example from the text to support it.

These sentence starters may help students:

I think that the… letter makes the most impact.

This is because the writer uses words like… to describe…

This makes them sound…

3 Understand how authors use sentences

Getting you thinking

Read the extract together as a class. Ask students what they notice about the length of the sentences in the passage. Did the short sentences slow down or speed up your reading?

How does it work?

It may be helpful to remind students what a sentence is, using this short explanation:

- A sentence begins with a capital letter and ends with a full stop – unless it is a question or an exclamation. Questions end with question marks. Got that? Exclamations end with exclamation marks. Like this!
- A sentence must contain a complete piece of information. It must have a *subject* (who or what it's about) and an *active verb* (a doing or being word).

Point out that the phrase 'The leader' is not a sentence. Nor is 'was still there'. But 'The leader was still there' is a perfect sentence.

Robert Westall uses a mixture of short and long sentences.

- The longer, more complex sentence beginning, 'If Harry made off…', shows that Harry's situation is complicated. He is thinking through his options.
- The short sentence, 'The leader had to be fixed', simply states his solution to the problem.

Now you try it

There is one sentence near the end which breaks the rules, because it has no subject or verb. Which one? What is the effect?

4 Understand how writers use dialogue

Getting you thinking

Read the passage together, if appropriate asking students to play the parts of the three characters.

How does it work?

Explain to students that good writers often follow the rule, 'Show, don't tell.' It is more interesting for readers to learn about characters from what they say or do than by the narrator just telling us 'Walkman and Fax were bullies who threatened other teenagers.'

Now you try it

Again read the passage aloud first to ensure understanding.

Development

In groups, ask students to 'hot seat' all the characters.

It may help students to gather some information about their character first by looking back over the two passages, or even by asking students to perform the two passages in groups of three – this time acting out the 'stage directions' given between the actual dialogue rather than reading them.

As an extension, ask students to write one sentence about their character. For example, to comment on Walkman, they could begin:

We can tell that Walkman is a bully because it says he 'grinned like a wolf' …

5 Identify different tenses

Getting you thinking

Read aloud and model how the past, present and future tenses are used in each extract.

Now you try it

Rewrite the 'present tense' extract opposite into the past tense.

Recap on the past tense by explaining that most verbs in the past tense end in '-ed', such as 'hurried' and 'challenged', but some have other endings. For example, you would say 'The trapeze artist *hung* in the air.' What would be the past tense versions of 'she swings…' and 'she holds her breath'?

Development

As an extension, get students to try out writing in the present and future tenses:

1 Ask your partner what their ideal future life would be, and what they want to achieve before getting old.

Then imagine that you can wave a magic wand to make their dreams come true. Predict a life for them in which they get everything they want. You could begin, *'At the age of 16, you will…'*

2 Then swap. This time, the person with the magic wand is looking into a crystal ball and 'seeing' the future now (in the present tense). They could begin *'You are 16. You are playing centre forward for…'*

> **Chapter 5 AF6 Identify and comment on writers' purposes and viewpoints, and the overall effect of the text on the reader**

1 Write and talk about the purpose of a text

How does it work?

When we look at a text we need to think about why it was written or produced. Explain to students that in the next activities they are going to work out what the purpose (or purposes) of one text might be and give some evidence for their ideas.

Now you try it

3 *Why do you think the filmmakers produced a website like this? Work with your partner to make a list of ideas.*

Encourage students to think of more than one reason why the website was created.

4 *Now point to three pieces of evidence in the text which show you that you're right.*

Again, encourage students to use technical language if they can.

2 Write and talk about the viewpoint of the writer

This lesson focuses on narrative perspective in fiction rather than the more straightforward viewpoint you might find in a non-fiction text, such as a newspaper article.

The lesson looks at John Boyne's novel, *The Boy in the Striped Pyjamas*, which deals with a harrowing historical event, the Holocaust, from the point of view of an innocent.

How does it work?

Explain to students that when stories are written in the **first person** from a **character's viewpoint**, we often find out more about what is going on in their head. We see only what they see. This can make us *empathise* with them.

Then explain that, in contrast, when stories are written in the **third person** from the **writer's viewpoint**, we can see what happens to several characters.

Now you try it

Begin by explaining to students that even when a writer writes in the third person, using their own voice to tell a story, they can still tell the story from one character's viewpoint.

Development

You will need small post-it notes for this activity.

As an extension, ask students to complete the following tasks:

1 Now you are going to comment further on the writer's viewpoint. Try answering this question in three or more sentences:

Which phrase tells you what the writer's viewpoint is in the passage from *The Boy in the Striped Pyjamas*?

You can use this structure to help you if you need it:

John Boyne is writing from the point of view of…
The phrase that tells me this is…
I chose this because…

2 Look at this example of a Level 4 answer. Point to where this student has identified the writer's **viewpoint**:

John Boyne is writing from the point of view of Bruno. One of the phrases that tells me this is 'all Bruno could see was an enormous pair of eyes staring back'. I chose this because it tells us what Bruno sees but not what the other boy saw.

3 And finally… point to the place in your writing where you have identified the writer's viewpoint. Do you need to rewrite any parts of your answer to make it clearer?

3 Use your understanding of viewpoint in your own writing

Getting you thinking

1 *With your partner, look at the opening page of a book you have been reading in your English lessons.*

Can you work out whether the story is
- *written from the writer's viewpoint*
- *written from a character's viewpoint?*

Help students by giving them these clues:

- **writer's viewpoint:** is the story told in the third person, using 'he' or 'she', as if the writer was describing what is happening?

- **character's viewpoint:** is the story told in the first person, using 'I', as if a character was speaking to you?

Development

You will need small post-it notes for this activity.

When students have finished writing their passage from Shmuel's viewpoint, ask them to swap their work with a partner. Do they need to redraft any of your writing to make sure that it is all from Shmuel's viewpoint?

Extension

You may want to explain to students why viewpoint is so important in *The Boy in the Striped Pyjamas*. John Boyne chooses to tell the story of the Holocaust through the eyes of a young German boy who doesn't fully understand what is happening – although we do.

4 Write and talk about the effect of a text on the reader

How does it work?

Explain to students that when an artist or a photographer creates a picture, they think about how they want the viewer to feel.

Tell them that when we look at a picture we 'read' it like a piece of written text. This means we interpret it and think about the decisions the artist has made in creating it.

Now you try it!

Look again at the pictures and decide which lion is most frightening. Think of three reasons for your choice.

Prompt students to think about why the lion looks frightening:

- Is it the way the lion is drawn / painted? (The style of the picture.) Is it like a cartoon? Or realistic? Or is it because it is a photo of a real lion?

- Is it the expression on the lion's face?
- Is it the lion's posture (how it is sitting / crouching / lying)?
- Is it the angle we are looking at the lion from? (above / below)
- Is it the way other people or animals in the picture react to it?

Share students' questions about the images.

Development activities

Read the verse aloud to students. You may need to explain why 'were' is used in the poem instead of 'was': because the poem is written in non-Standard English in a particular 'voice'.

Draw the discussion to a conclusion by reminding students that writers choose their words carefully to achieve their purpose. This might be to make us think or feel something, or to create a picture in our minds.

5 Write and talk about the effect of a writer's word choices

Getting you thinking

Read the verses aloud, explaining they are part of a poem that was written to be spoken aloud to make people laugh.

Ask for students' responses to the way the poem sounds when read aloud:

● Did it sound like the way your teacher normally speaks? Why / why not?

● Would the poem sound funnier in a different accent? Which one?

● Do all the rhymes make the poem sound serious or comical?

● How do you think the writer wants us to feel about Albert and his family?

● How do you think the writer want us to feel about Albert's death? (That it was funny / deeply moving / a terrible tragedy / his own fault?)

How does it work?

(William Wallace was a Scottish general who fought a fierce war of independence against England in 1296 until he was captured and executed in 1305. And yet, as a name for a lion, it is funny.)

Draw attention to the way that phrases like 'swallowed the little lad whole' make the story sound like a picture postcard joke, rather than the violent and messy event it would be in real life.

Now you try it

You may want to prompt students to reflect on the comical tone or mood of the poem. Does this affect the way we read the actual words of the poem? For example, do students think the writer really sees Albert as a 'brave little feller'?

Chapter 6 AF7 Relate texts to their social, cultural and historical traditions

---

1 Identify different time, place and social settings in texts

Getting you thinking

Read the passage aloud with students first, then ask them to work in groups of three to carry out the role play.

How does it work?

Explain to students that in any book we read, we need to understand where the story is set, and to think about how that time, place or society might be different from our own.

Tell students that the book is based on true events in America in the second half of the

nineteenth century. The Apache were a tribe feared for their skill and courage in battle.

Explain that the Apache training happens in a real – though past – world.

Emphasise to students that the Apache training doesn't make sense in a modern school setting. These are not lessons we would be allowed – or need – to learn today.

Now you try it

Read the extract together as a class, then ask students to work in pairs to find three clues that Nat has not woken up in contemporary England.

---

2 Identify character and setting in texts

Getting you thinking

Read the passage aloud with students and help them work through the questions.

How does it work?

Draw out with students how we know where the story is set and who the character is:

● The **setting** is the first class compartment of a train. It is also a smoking carriage, so the story must be set in the past, before smoking in enclosed public spaces was banned in the UK (July 2007), but after trains were invented in 1804 (first steam locomotive Merthyr Tydfil, Wales, downhill to Abercynnon, 1804). The train is passing through Somerset, and on a long journey. Therefore (b) is the best answer.

- We meet a **character**, Mr Justice Wargrave. The words 'Justice' and 'lately retired from the bench' tell us that he is a recently retired Judge. We learn what newspaper he reads and what he is interested in – the 'political news'. Not bad for one sentence!
- The **mood** – how the characters and setting are **presented** – is a bit harder to pin down. Cosy and old-fashioned are probably the best, though not the only, descriptions.

The setting is the first class compartment of a train, in England, in the twentieth-century.

The character we meet is Mr Justice Wargrave, a retired judge.

The paragraph takes you into a peaceful, cosy and old fashioned world.

Now you try it

Read the passage aloud with students at least once to ensure understanding.

Development

*In pairs, focus on either **character** or **setting**. Find as much information as you can from the text about your strand.*

Help students by giving them these questions as prompts:

- **Character:** What do we learn from the way the character acts, or what he says about himself and how he feels?
- **Setting:** What details suggest to you that this story might be set in the past? Think about what the character is wearing, for instance.

3 Compare texts in the same genre

Getting You Thinking

Read the Celia Rees extract aloud with the class. Ask students who they think is telling the story. A hardened pirate? A first-timer?

How does it work?

Did students notice the pirate words and phrases:
- 'The prize'
- 'Reckless boldness'
- 'Men who seem to laugh in the face of death itself'.

Did students notice the pirate story features:
- telling the story in the first person.
- the terror, weaponry and violence
- the setting: at sea in sailing ships.

Draw out that the pirate words and phrases all suggest a swashbuckling attitude to crime on the high seas. And 'if the *prize* offered resistance, it was kill or be killed' is a pirate word. Naval seamen would say the 'enemy' and fight to the death. Merchant seamen would not kill, be killed, nor steal.

The setting is also a giveaway. 'We boarded the **prize** through **blinding billows**' is a 'pirate' setting – exciting and dangerous. Real pirates still operate today but pirate *stories* tend to be set in the days of sailing ships, like this. Two ships

splintering together makes the setting clear – violence at sea.

Conclude that, overall, pirates are described as bold, exciting sea-criminals, overcoming fear, laughing at death, onboard sailing ships.

Now you try it

Explain to students that Stevenson 'wrote the book' as far as pirate stories are concerned with his famous *Ar Jim lad* parrot-on-the shoulder Long John Silver character, pictured above. (His ship sets sail from Bristol, a famous seafaring centre at the time, and his traditional pirate accent is a mixture of West Country and Irish.)

Feed back students ideas. Did they notice these pirate words and phrases?
- fo'c's'le
- Captain
- hideous scar
- missing three fingers
- cutlass

Ask students to look up any unfamiliar words in a dictionary and note down their meaning.

Development

Raid the drama cupboard for some pirate props: a locked treasure chest, an eye-patch, a map that has been torn in half.

Working in pairs, students should explain where each one comes from – and the story behind it. For example:

> A: *this eye patch belonged to One Eye O'Keef, the most feared pirate in the Caribbean.*
>
> B: *(adds an idea) He was famous for eating seagulls raw for breakfast, washed down with rum.*
>
> A: *Yes, do you remember when…*

Remind students to think about pirate settings – the high seas – and pirate words and phrases.

Extension

Ask students to design the front cover of a new pirate book called *Pirates Ahoy*. They should include the treasure chest, the eye patch or the map in their design.

4 Identify characters and settings in texts from different times

Getting you thinking

Read the passage aloud to students.

How does it work?

Explain to students that the passage describes the real experiences of a British helicopter pilot, Ed Macy, in the present-day conflict in Afghanistan. (The book concerns his 2006 posting.)

He and his helicopter crew are told over their radio that they need to go and check on a possibly hostile situation.

The **characters** are the narrator, the helicopter pilot Carl, and the other helicopter pilots we hear speaking to them by radio.

The **setting** is inside an Apache helicopter gunship. In this passage, the narrator is the helicopter gunner.

The advanced technology (FLIR, radio) suggests that this is a modern, hi-tech battle.

Now you try it

Read the poem to students.

Ask them to look for similar clues as to when the poem is set. Draw out that:

- The **characters** are the Light Brigade of the title, the 'six hundred' who 'fought so well'. Explain that the Light Brigade was the elite 'light' cavalry section of the British army. 'Light' meant lightly armoured men on fast horses of less than fourteen hands. Heavy cavalry were heavily armoured and rode the largest horses. Tanks and armoured cars have now replaced both.

- The **setting** is the battlefield, with the cannons firing shells and shot from left, right and in front of the cavalry.

- The **presentation** comes through in phrases like 'the jaws of Death', 'the mouth of Hell' and 'horse and hero'. The writer admires the courage shown. But there is also – in 'all that was left of them' – a note of reproach. Cavalry shouldn't fight artillery.

Students might be interested to know that in addition to medium-range explosive shells and short-range canister shot, the cannons had a long-range capacity to fire cannon balls. These did terrible damage, often taking off heads and bits of horses and men. But, being long-range, you could at least see them coming and dodge them.

Development

You will need a digital camera for this activity. It would be great if you could actually add the captions to students' photos on the computer, so they have a finished product to show for their work.

Notes

Notes

Notes